# 'DEAREST EMMIE'

## Thomas Hardy's Letters
## to His First Wife

*The editor of this book is the author of* :

HARDY OF WESSEX : a Centennial Biography : New York, Columbia University Press, 1940

THE FIRST HUNDRED YEARS OF THOMAS HARDY : a Bibliography : Waterville, Colby College Press, 1942

HARDY MUSIC : Colby, 1944

HARDY IN AMERICA : Colby, 1946

HARDY AND THE LADY FROM MADISON SQUARE : Waterville, Colby College Press, 1952

THE RISE AND FALL OF JAMES RIPLEY OSGOOD (Hardy's Publisher) : Waterville, Colby College Press, 1959

*The editor of this book has also edited* :

HARDY'S 'LOST' NOVEL : Baltimore, The Johns Hopkins Press, 1935

HARDY'S TESS OF THE D'URBERVILLES : New York, Harper & Brothers, 1935

HARDY'S FAR FROM THE MADDING CROWD : Oxford University Press, 1937

HARDY'S UNCOLLECTED TALES : Colby College Press, 1940

HARDY'S THREE WAYFARERS : New York, Scholars' Facsimiles, 1943

HARDY'S TESS OF THE D'URBERVILLES : New York, Random House, 1951

HARDY'S LETTERS : Waterville, Colby College Press, 1954

HARDY'S JUDE THE OBSCURE : New York, Harper & Brothers, 1957

HARDY'S THE WOODLANDERS : New York, Harper & Brothers, 1958

HARDY'S FAR FROM THE MADDING CROWD : New York, Holt, Rinehart & Winston, 1959

HARDY'S TESS OF THE D'URBERVILLES : New York, Dodd, Mead & Co., 1960

THOMAS HARDY IN THE 1880's

# 'DEAREST EMMIE'

## Thomas Hardy's Letters
## to His First Wife

EDITED BY
### CARL J. WEBER

LONDON
MACMILLAN & CO LTD
NEW YORK · ST MARTIN'S PRESS
1963

MACMILLAN AND COMPANY LIMITED
*St Martin's Street London WC2*
*also Bombay Calcutta Madras Melbourne*

THE MACMILLAN COMPANY OF CANADA LIMITED
*Toronto*

ST MARTIN'S PRESS INC
*New York*

B 6 3 0 9 5 3 3

PRINTED IN GREAT BRITAIN

216512    General

# PREFACE

THIS book contains the text of all the letters that are known to have survived from the larger number of letters which Hardy wrote to his first wife. He met her in March 1870 ; they were married in September 1874. During their engagement, as Mrs. Hardy later recorded, 'My Architect came two or three times a year . . . to visit me. . . . In the intervals of his visits we corresponded.' Apparently none of those letters of 1870–1874 have survived — neither his to her nor hers to him. Hardy himself rescued two sentences which his bride-to-be wrote him in July 1874, when he was in the throes of composing *Far from the Madding Crowd*. Emma wrote : 'My work, unlike your work of writing, does not occupy my true mind much. . . . Your novel seems sometimes like a child all your own and none of me.' He copied her words into his notebook.

After their marriage, the Hardys spent the next ten years in a variety of rented lodgings, and at last, in June 1885, they moved into a house of their own — Max Gate — a mile out of Dorchester on the road to Wareham, a house which Hardy himself had designed and had supervised the construction of during the eighteen months required for its building. During those ten years of life in rented lodgings, the Hardys were rarely separated, and if any letters were written during that time by either one to the other, those letters have not survived.

The construction of Max Gate, however, opened a new chapter in Hardy's life. His fame as the author of *Far from the*

*Madding Crowd, The Return of the Native*, and *The Trumpet-Major* had led to membership in the Savile Club in London, and to frequent invitations to dinners, teas, and 'crushes' (as Hardy called them) during the London 'season'. But not until he became a landowner and the proprietor of his own dwelling were he and Mrs. Hardy invited to be house-guests for extended stays in other homes. Early in 1885 Lord and Lady Portsmouth invited the Hardys to Eggesford House in North Devon. They accepted the invitation and a date was fixed for the visit. When the time came, however, Mrs. Hardy found herself ill and unable to go. Hardy accordingly went alone and thus occasioned the resumption of the correspondence which his marriage in 1874 had ended. Once resumed, the letter-writing was to continue (with occasional intervals) for the next twenty-six years. It is this quarter-century record of a famous author's marital domesticity that is here offered to the reader.

Enough has already been published in various quarters about the relationship of the first Mrs. Hardy and her famous poet-novelist husband to make it certain that these surviving letters will be read with avid interest. Rumour and gossip — if not partizanship and downright malice — have had half a century and more in which to stir up curiosity and set tongues to buzzing. On January 18, 1916 — to take just one example — the second Mrs. Hardy wrote to Rebekah Owen : 'I keep a diary . . . but when I remember the *awful* diary the first Mrs. T. H. kept (which he burned) full of venom, hatred, and abuse of him and his family, I am afraid to do more than chronicle facts'.

In the shadow of this report of venom, hatred, and abuse, and of other reports like it from other sources, we can count ourselves fortunate that at least seventy-four letters have survived to give us some opportunity to judge for ourselves.

# Preface

These letters can free us, at least to some extent, from the dangers of relying on irresponsible gossip and malicious rumour. Newman once remarked : 'Biographers varnish, they assign motives, they conjecture feelings, they interpret Lord Burleigh's nod, but contemporary letters are facts'. These letters of Hardy's are facts ; they constitute a more reliable key to an understanding of the man who wrote them to his wife than do the guesses and surmises of his critics and biographers.

Unfortunately, we have only one side of the correspondence. Emma's letters to her husband have not survived. If Hardy ever kept them, they probably went into the sweeping destruction of his papers which he undertook in the later years of his life. On May 7, 1919, he wrote to Sir George Douglas : 'I have not been doing much — mainly destroying papers of the last thirty or forty years'.

Hardy's own side of the correspondence casts a useful and welcome searchlight upon his own character, and helps us to a clearer understanding of the reason why a visitor to Max Gate — one who knew Hardy and his first wife very well — could write in 1912 to another visitor : 'Thank you very much for your letter and refutation of Mrs. Hardy's charges against her poor old patient husband. She is a queer woman and I never thought her quite right in the upper storey !' The visitor here quoted was Miss Teresa Charlotte Fetherstonhaugh-Frampton, of Moreton, Dorset. Her family — the Framptons — had for seven centuries owned a great part of 'Egdon Heath'.

It will, of course, not do to expect too much of Hardy's letters. As Professor Frederick A. Pottle has remarked : 'Hardy husbanded his genius and never intentionally spilled any of it in letters'. This is another way of saying that Thomas Hardy was not like Samuel Johnson in thinking that letters were a branch of literature — 'epistolick art' — and Hardy would never have boasted to Emma, as Johnson once boasted to Mrs. Thrale : 'If our correspondence were printed, I am sure posterity would say that I am a good writer'. No one would say that about Hardy, if one had only his letters to judge him by. He was business-like, brief, clear, but in his letters he never made any effort to be charming or graceful or 'intimate'. Other men have done so — Thackeray, for example, and Charles Lamb, and Edward FitzGerald — but Hardy does not belong in their company.

Why then print the letters ? Because they provide the most reliable evidence available to help us arrive at a clear under-standing of the atmosphere at Max Gate in which Hardy lived. It was this atmosphere that eventually developed into the 'climate' in which the 'Poems of 1912–13' were written. These poems, the 'veteris vestigia flammae', and others to be associated with them, *are* literature — great literature — and no sincere admirer of the treasures of English poetry can afford to ignore them. The present editor now has in process of prep-aration an edition of *Hardy's Love Poems*, in which all the poems inspired by, or addressed to, or more remotely occasioned by, Emma Lavinia Gifford will be brought together and given the unity and focus they have not as yet enjoyed. But before this can be done, some clarification of Hardy's experience is desirable — necessary, in fact — if one is to approach the poems with anything like full understanding and appreciation. These letters afford the opportunity for that clarification.

The original holographs on which this book is based are now in the Hardy Room of the Dorset County Museum in Dorchester, where Curator R. N. R. Peers has placed me in his debt by his unfailing kindness and courtesy during the time when I was at work in the Hardy Room. These letters are here printed by permission of the Trustees of the Hardy copy-right, Lloyds Bank Ltd., London, and Miss I. Cooper Willis. I am happy to express my gratitude to Miss Willis for past kindness, assistance, and encouragement.

In transcribing Hardy's letters, I have felt that there was nothing to be gained by annoying the reader by printing 'shd.' or 'sh[oul]d' when it is perfectly clear that Hardy meant 'should'. He wrote rapidly and abbreviated many words ; for example, affectionately, afternoon, church, could, exhibition, husband, lord, park, perhaps, said, should, Thursday, Wednesday, and would ; but in no case is there any doubt as to what he meant. I have therefore silently expanded the novelist's abbreviations. Whenever parentheses appear in the letters, they are Hardy's own. Whenever square brackets appear, they enclose insertions by the editor. Some of the dates have been thus inserted. For example, in Letter No. 14, the date ' [May 23, 1892]' is supplied by the editor, the contents of the letter serving to authenticate this dating. Whenever there is any doubt about the conjectured ascription (as, for example, with Letter No. 21), that fact is indicated by the use of question-marks, *e.g.* '[? April 4, 1895 ?]'. The doubtful cases are very few.

Editorial quotations from Hardy's verse are made by permission of Macmillan & Company, Ltd., publishers of *Collected Poems* by Thomas Hardy ; and for this permission as well as for other kindnesses and courtesies I make grateful acknowledgement of the assistance rendered me by Messrs. R. F. Allen and T. M. Farmiloe in the Macmillan office. I am also indebted to my wife, Clara Carter Weber, for help in copying, in criticizing, and otherwise furthering this project. A grant-in-aid from the American Council of Learned Societies enabled us to go to England, and this assistance is gratefully acknowledged.

CARL J. WEBER

COLBY COLLEGE,
WATERVILLE, MAINE, U.S.A.

ix

# CONTENTS

———

FRONTISPIECE

THOMAS HARDY IN THE 1880's

# INTRODUCTION

THOMAS HARDY saw Emma Lavinia Gifford for the first time
on March 7, 1870. He never forgot the date. More than half
a century later he wrote in his notebook : 'March 7, 1924 :
E. first met 54 years ago'. He could (and often did) forget
her birthday, but he never failed to recall that on

> this day of the year
> (What rainbow-rays embow it !)
> We met, strangers confessed,
> But parted — blest.

These lines from his poem 'Looking at a Picture on an Anniversary' were written on March 7, 1913, a few months after
her death.

It may doubtless be safely assumed that most readers of this
volume will come to it already equipped with some knowledge
of what events had preceded that eventful day in March 1870
in the lives of the two persons who then met ; but for those
readers who lack that knowledge, or who may feel a desire for
the editor to wield a duster over a clouded surface of memory,
a brief summary of those events may prove useful.

Hardy was born on June 2, 1840, in a cottage at Higher
Bockhampton, Dorset, three miles east of Dorchester. He
grew up there on the edge of the extensive tract of then-
uncultivated land to which he was later to give the name
Egdon Heath. He was a frail child, small (even as a grown
man he was only 5 feet 7 inches tall), and not until he was
eight years old was he sent to school. He had only eight years

of formal education, seven of them spent in Dorchester schools to which he walked three miles daily, and three miles home again. At the age of sixteen he was apprenticed to a Dorchester architect, and when he was twenty-one he moved to London and found employment with Arthur Blomfield. Hardy remained in London until 1867. Then, finding life in the metropolis increasingly unattractive and a career as an architect increasingly uninviting, he returned to Bockhampton and there experimented with literary composition while living with his parents.

He had written some poetry while in London but had been unable to get any of it published. After his return to Dorset, he tried his hand at prose fiction, and by the time he made his memorable trip to Cornwall in 1870 he had completed two novels. Neither of these had as yet attained publication, and one of them (the first) was never to appear in print. The second, however, was published in 1871, at his own expense, and this was followed by eight others, so that by the time Hardy and his wife moved into Max Gate in 1885 he was known as the author of nine books, of which *Far from the Madding Crowd* had proved the most successful. This novel ran in *The Cornhill* throughout the year 1874, and it was this success that enabled Hardy to marry Miss Gifford on September 17th of that year.

At the time when he penned the first letter in the present volume, Hardy was engaged in the composition of *The Mayor of Casterbridge*. He wrote the last page of his manuscript on April 17, 1885. This novel (his tenth to be published) appeared in print in May 1886.

EMMA LAVINIA GIFFORD was born in Plymouth on November 24, 1840, and the first eighteen years of her life were spent there. Many years later she was to write of her girlhood : 'My home was a most intellectual one and not only so but one of exquisite home-training and refinement — alas the difference the loss of these amenities and gentlenesses has made to me !' But this 'recollection', written when she was seventy, does not tell the whole story. Her father, John Attersoll Gifford, was a violin-playing solicitor, subject to 'occasional outbursts of drink'. He had 'retired' early, and during the eighteen years of Emma's girlhood in Plymouth he was supported by 'Grandmamma Gifford', who lived with the family. She had an income of seven hundred pounds a year, which (as Emma noted) 'was considered a good income in those days'. When the grandmother died, the Giffords moved to Bodmin, Cornwall, in order to 'retrench' — the old lady's estate being divided into so many parts that Emma's father could no longer afford to keep up the house in Plymouth. Emma herself eventually inherited two hundred and twenty pounds in Plymouth stock.

After the move to Bodmin, Emma's sister, Helen Catherine, found the home-life dull. She accordingly tried to support herself away from home as a governess ; but after six months she returned to Bodmin and induced Emma to take her place. But after another six months, Emma too had had enough of 'governessing' (her word for it), and when her sister married the elderly Reverend Caddell Holder, the rector of St. Juliot, North Cornwall, Emma went with her and lived with the Holders at The Rectory. There she helped her sister with the house affairs, 'visiting parish folk and playing the harmonium on Sundays'.

The church at St. Juliot had suffered from long neglect. The tower was cracked, the pew-ends were rotten, and ivy hung from the roof-timbers. By 1869 it was clear that something *had* to be done. Mr. Holder consulted John Hicks, the Dorchester architect under whom Hardy had served his six-year apprenticeship ; but before the church-restoration at St.

Juliot was begun, John Hicks died. His practice was purchased by G. R. Crickmay, an architect in Weymouth ; and when Crickmay found himself burdened with more work than he could handle, he called upon Thomas Hardy for help. In February 1870 he asked Hardy : 'Can you go into Cornwall for me, to take a plan and particulars of a church I am about to rebuild there ?'

Hardy agreed to go, and as soon as he had dispatched the manuscript of his novel *Desperate Remedies* to London, he set out for Cornwall. The date was March 7, 1870. On his arrival at St. Juliot, Miss Gifford met him at the door of the rectory. Each was then in his (or her) thirtieth year. Years later Hardy wrote :

> She opened the door of Romance to me,
> The door from a cell
> I had known too well,
> Too long, till then, and was fain to flee.

> She opened the door of a Love to me,
> That passed the wry
> World-welters by
> As far as the arching blue the lea.

They were married in 1874, and their united lives during the next ten years were spent in Surbiton, Westbourne Grove, Swanage, Yeovil, Sturminster Newton, Upper Tooting, and Wimborne. During these years Hardy wrote and published the novels already referred to. Finally, in June 1883, the Hardys moved to Shire Hall Lane, Dorchester, and there they resided while Max Gate was under construction. To this address Hardy sent the first letters of the present collection.

## LETTER NO. 1

Eggesford House, Wembworthy, N. Devon.
Friday March 13, [18]85.

My dearest Em,

I arrived at Eggesford Station a little after 4, and found there Lord Portsmouth's brougham waiting to take me up to the house, so there was no trouble at all. The scenery here is lovely and the house very handsome — not an enormous one — but telling on account of its position, which is on a hill in the park.[1] I have had tea with Lady Portsmouth and the ladies — the only members of the family at home — Lord Portsmouth not having returned from hunting yet (6 p.m.). The young ladies[2] are very attentive, and interested in what I tell them — Lady Portsmouth charges them to take care of me — and goes away to her parish people etc. — altogether a delightful household. There are [other] ladies here too, visiting, but of course I have only had a glimpse [of them] as yet. They sympathise with you — and Lady Portsmouth says you *must* come when you are well. I am now in the library writing this. I should say that a married daughter, Lady Rosamond Christie, I think she is, who is here, strikes me as a particularly sensible woman. If Lady Portsmouth's orders are to be carried out my room will be like a furnace — she is so particularly anxious that I should not take cold, etc. The drawing room is lined with oak panels from a

[1] Eggesford is about a dozen miles north-east of Okehampton, Devon.
[2] Lady Dorothea, Lady Camilla, and their cousin Lady Winifred Herbert.

B                               I

monastery. When I arrived the schoolchildren were practising singing in the hall, for Sunday in Church.

In haste (as you will believe)

Yours ever
Том.

## LETTER NO. 2

29 Montague St. [London]
[Saturday, May 16, 1885.]

My dearest Emmie,

I went to Lady Carnarvon's last night — and was very well received — indeed they all seemed more friendly than on the first occasion.[1] I rather wish I had known the contents of her note, as she evidently wants the address we are staying or going to stay at — and I did not give it her. If I call Monday, and leave it pencilled on my cards will that be sufficient do you think — or ought I to see her in making such a call ? The Portsmouth sisters were there — except Lady Camilla. You were much enquired for — Lady Dorothea, Lady Margaret, Lady Winifred Herbert, and Lady Carnarvon herself, all expressing sorrow that you could not come. Lady Portsmouth's daughters are at present staying at their aunt's — Lady Portsmouth comes to town to-day or Monday. There were more people — rather more — present than the other Friday,[2] but more of a mixed kind — not quite so select. Among others there was Mrs. Oliphant, to whom I was introduced. I don't care a bit for her — and you lose nothing

*Social women*

[1] Two weeks earlier, Mrs. Hardy had been present with her husband in London and on Friday, May 1, had attended a Carnarvon party given at the time of a 'private view' of the art exhibition at the Royal Academy. She had soon after returned to Dorchester to arrange for their moving to London for the 'season'.

[2] On Saturday evening, May 2, the annual dinner of the Royal Academy of Arts was held, inaugurating the Exhibition which was opened to the public on Monday, May 4.

*doesn't well here*

by not knowing her. She is propriety and primness incarnate.[1] Robert Browning was there — and Lady Carnarvon's mother, to whom she introduced me. Also Mrs. Jeune the irrepressible — she was very cool — I think because you have not called — and I could not get to tell her why.[2] However a little delay will do her no harm. Nearly all the ladies were wearing the same dresses as before, Lady Winifred's divine blue looking decidedly crumpled about the neck — the stick-up ruff, I mean, not so well as when we saw it [two weeks ago] in all its new glory. Lady Margaret was in black lace, with gloves between salmon and buff, and a dull red fan and necklace of brilliants — and between black ornaments — dress low. Both the sisters tell me in confidence that they feel shy of meeting so many people, having been shut up in the country so long. Lady Winifred started away at the tea-pouring — complaining bitterly of the heaviness of the

[1] Hardy's dislike of Mrs. M. O. W. Oliphant was prophetic. Ten years later, just after the publication of *Jude the Obscure*, she wrote an article entitled 'The Anti-Marriage League'. It appeared in *Blackwood's* (159 : 135-149), January 1896. This article did not improve Hardy's fondness for her. In his April 1912 preface to *Jude the Obscure* he referred to 'the screaming of a poor lady in *Blackwood*'.

[2] Mrs. Jeune (later Lady Jeune, later still Lady St. Helier) is mentioned so often in these letters that it will help the reader if some information about her is here set down. She had previously married Colonel J. Constantine Stanley ; their daughter Dorothy was still a little girl when Hardy first became acquainted with her mother. After Colonel Stanley's death, Mrs. Stanley married Francis Henry Jeune, the son of the Bishop of Peterborough. Mr. Jeune was knighted in 1892, and as Sir Francis held the post of Judge-Advocate-General. In February 1894 Hardy gave him a copy of *Life's Little Ironies*, having heard from his lips many an 'ironical' divorce-court report out of Sir Francis's legal experience. Sir Francis Jeune was later created Lord St. Helier. In July 1896 his lordship's stepdaughter, Dorothy Stanley, married Henry Allhusen (1867–1928) of Stoke Court, Stoke Poges, Buckinghamshire ; Hardy attended her wedding. He quotes her in Letter No. 19. In 1918 he wrote for her a war 'Appeal for Mrs. Allhusen's Canteens'. Another of Mrs. Jeune's daughters became Mrs. Brodick, to whom Hardy presented a copy of *The Dynasts* in 1904. In 1909 Lady St. Helier published her *Memories of Fifty Years*.

teapot, which was an enormous one. I forgot to include Murray Smith among those present — he was very warm.[1]

I am going to ask [our landlady] Miss Stokoe to-day about a sitting-room — but whether we arrange [to take it] or not will make no difference, as I am in the bedroom you had — so that you can arrive at any time. I should think Tuesday would do. Will you bring the flexible map of London. I have been confined all the morning by a dreadful headache — owing to some soup — but it is going off. Fitzgerald Molloy ('Court Life Below Stairs') met me in the British Museum reading room yesterday. He is an impulsive rather interesting Irishman. Shall we ask him to call ? This we can settle when you come. I am going to write to Weston now.

Yours affectionately ever<br>Tom.

[P.S. :] Will you caution the servants about turning on and off the gas.

   Fill up [a] form at the Post Office for letters etc. to be sent on *here.*

*  *  *

[There now occurs a gap of five years in this correspondence. The absence of letters during this period is probably best explained by the likelihood that Hardy and Emmie were rarely separated. In June 1885 they moved into Max Gate, and shortly thereafter received a call from Robert Louis Stevenson and his American wife. This call gives us an opportunity for an early glimpse of the Max Gate couple ; for on September 10, 1885, Mrs. Stevenson wrote to her mother-in-law : 'Did I tell you that we saw Hardy the novelist at Dorchester ? A

<hr>

[1] Hardy had met George Murray Smith in 1874, shortly before his firm, Smith, Elder & Co., became Hardy's publishers. By this date (1885) that firm had published four of the Wessex novels : *Far from the Madding Crowd, The Hand of Ethelberta, The Return of the Native,* and *The Trumpet-Major.*

pale, gentle, frightened little man, that one felt an instinctive
tenderness for, with a wife — ugly is no word for it ! — who
said "Whatever shall we do ?" I had never heard a human
being say it before.' During the five-year period that followed
the move into Max Gate, Hardy published three more books :
*The Mayor of Casterbridge* (1886), *The Woodlanders* (1887),
and *Wessex Tales* (1888). The second of these three gives us a
further opportunity for a glimpse through the windows of
Max Gate, for in *The Woodlanders* Hardy's hero Giles Winterborne meditates on a subject that cropped up with increasing
frequency in Hardy's home, and in Chapter 39 Winterborne
may be suspected of expressing some of his creator's own
thoughts : 'All night did Winterborne think over the un-
satisfactory ending of a pleasant time. . . . He feared anew
that they could never be happy together. . . . She was accomplished : he was unrefined. It was the original difficulty,
which he was too thoughtful to recklessly ignore, as some men
would have done in his place.' Not until after Winterborne
had died was it brought home forcefully to Grace's mind (in
Chapter 45 of *The Woodlanders*) 'how little acquirements and
culture weigh beside sterling personal character'. During the
period we are here dealing with, Emma Hardy signed her
name in a copy of *The Woodlanders*, but there is nothing to
tell us whether she saw any significance in the page on which
her husband had balanced 'culture' against 'sterling personal
character'. It remained for Professor Samuel C. Chew many
years later to note the significance of the admiration which
Hardy had so obviously lavished upon a man like Winterborne,
a man 'with courage, resourcefulness, patience, endurance,
clear-sightedness, tenderness, tolerance, forbearance, and un-
selfishness'. Chew declared that the elaborate care Hardy had
taken in the portrayal of Giles Winterborne (and of others like
him : Gabriel Oak, for example) provides 'the proper answer
to the foolish and uncritical opinion that Hardy is scornful of
human nature'. The reader may have noticed, however, that

a man with howsoever sterling a character could still write to his wife : 'Fill up [a] form at the Post Office', with never a 'please' or a 'thank you'.

[In 1890 Mrs. Hardy's father died — an event which accounts for the mourning border round the next letter which Hardy addressed to his wife.]

LETTER NO. 3

Savile Club, 107, Piccadilly, [London] W.
Thursday [July 24, 1890].

My dearest Em,

I hope to return either Saturday or Monday — the latter probably. I lunched at Mrs. Jeune's to-day. She is going into the country from Saturday to Monday and wants me to come and stay with her on the latter day. But I have told her November or December would suit best : I have been there so much lately that I don't want to bore her — and it is getting so warm here too. The Charity performance for her fund went off very well yesterday — and Miss Rehan read my verses : [1] I was not there myself. The *Daily News* says they are spirited ; the *Globe* that they are poor stuff. I think it is all right with the *Graphic* — as they really don't themselves know what it is I have written, apparently : one of the directors having read the first proofs in mistake for the second.[2]

[1] 'Lines Spoken by Miss Ada Rehan at the Lyceum Theatre, July 23, 1890, at a performance on behalf of Mrs. Jeune's Holiday Fund for City Children.' Hardy wrote these lines at the Savile Club at midnight on the 22nd.

[2] A day previously, Hardy had called at the *Graphic* office and there the editor, Arthur Locker, had told him that 'the directors' objected to his stories about the Noble Dames. Hardy's reaction (noted in *Early Life*, p. 297, where he erroneously dates the call as June 23) was : 'Here's a pretty job ! Must smooth down these Directors somehow I suppose.' He apparently did ; for the *Graphic* published 'A Group of Noble Dames', Christmas 1890.

*Letter No. 4*

I told Mrs. Jeune briefly, of your father's death — and she was very sympathetic.[1]

Ever yours affectionately,

Tom.

## LETTER NO. 4

My dearest Em,

The journey [up from Dorchester] was without incident. There was a fog when I arrived : which since my coming to the Club has thickened to blackness. London is London still — that's the impression first received in the streets. Men are reading the papers everywhere. The woman Peachey or Wheeler has been found guilty.[2] I have just had some tea and toast.

Ever affectionately,

Tom.

[P.S. :] I got a room all right at the West Central Hotel. If the Christmas *Graphic* comes will you send on one copy to Mrs. Childs (Lindisfarne, Weymouth).[3]

[1] Emma needed no elucidation of her husband's word 'briefly', for neither Hardy nor his wife ever forgot Mr. Gifford's opposition to their marriage. At this late date there is no way of proving or disproving the report that Gifford denounced Hardy as a 'base churl' for daring to wish to marry into the Gifford family, but it seems clear that one visit to Bodmin (in 1872) was enough, for Emma as well as for Hardy. Thereafter they met elsewhere — if not at St. Juliot, then at Bath or in London. Their marriage took place in London, at St. Peter's, Elgin Avenue, Paddington. Hardy's poem, 'Near Lanivet, 1872', records how Emma had leaned on 'a stunted handpost' near her father's house 'like one . . . bodily crucified', and ends with Hardy's own pained 'Alas, alas !'

[2] Mrs. Pearcey, alias Mary E. Wheeler, was hanged for murder on December 22, 1890.

[3] The *Graphic* contained 'A Group of Noble Dames', six of the stories in the book of that title published in May 1891. The 'great picture' was

7

You can leave out the great picture if it makes folding difficult.

## LETTER NO. 5

Savile Club, 107 Piccadilly, W.
Friday afternoon [December 5, 1890].

My dearest Em,

I have just had a letter from Mrs. Jeune (in addition to the one you sent on, which I briefly answered) saying that she will be delighted to have me *Monday* [December 8]. I think therefore I will go to her, since I had planned to do so. Will you post on anything to me here up to Sunday night — and I will let you know if longer.

The passing of the Copyright Bill by the American House of Representatives [on December 3] is a surprise to everybody. It is sure to pass the Senate, Osgood says (I have seen him to-day).[1] The Senate is virtually the

a coloured reproduction measuring 12″ × 16½″. It filled pages 18 and 19, and if Mrs. Hardy followed his directions and left the picture out, with it went part of Hardy's story, printed on page 20.

[1] James Ripley Osgood, an American by birth, had spent thirty years (1855–1885) as a publisher in Boston, Massachusetts, U.S.A., during which time he had (in 1873) paid $375 for the 'advance sheets' of the *Cornhill Magazine* in which Hardy's *Far from the Madding Crowd* was to appear. Osgood's attempt to become Hardy's American publisher was frustrated by the lack of an international copyright law in those days, but after Osgood had gone bankrupt in Boston (in 1885), he became an agent for Harper & Brothers and (in May 1886) was sent by them to London, where (in 1887) he was instrumental in steering *The Woodlanders* into the pages of *Harper's Bazar* (in those days it was spelled without the doubled 'a'), where it appeared in weekly instalments from May 15, 1886, to April 9, 1887. Upon the passing of the American Copyright Bill of which Hardy speaks, Osgood set up his own publishing house in London, and this led, in time, to his firm, Osgood, McIlvaine & Co., becoming (in 1891) Hardy's publishers. Unfortunately, Osgood died soon after this (see Letter No. 14), and when his contract with Osgood expired, Hardy transferred all his business to Macmillan & Company, where it remains. For further information about Hardy's relations with James R. Osgood, see *The Rise and Fall of James Ripley Osgood*, by Carl J. Weber (Waterville, Maine : Colby College Press, 1959).

American house of lords. It will probably become law next July — and nobody knows what difference it may make to us English authors.[1]

I attended the dinner to Thomas — It was an *enormous* affair — M.P.s and Q.C.s, authors, etc.

Probably I shall just save the Copyright of *Tess* in America — owing to delay. If all goes well how fortunate.[2]

Ever yours affectionately

TOM.

[P.S. :] If I should change my plan, and come [home earlier], it will of course make no difference.

[1] It made a vast difference to Hardy, and contributed not a little to his leaving an estate of approximately £90,000 at his death.

[2] This remains, I think, the only instance of Hardy's recognizing 'how fortunate' he was. He was much more in the habit of thinking how *un-*fortunate he was. In this matter of Copyright, he had reason to recall how, on May 11, 1875, he had gone with Charles Reade, as a delegation from the Association to Protect the Rights of Authors, to call on Prime Minister Disraeli, to seek his help in effecting changes in the copyright law. Shortly after this, Hardy had met the American minister, James Russell Lowell, in London, and had talked with him about the great desirability of changes in the international copyright situation. Lowell was sufficiently impressed with Hardy's remarks to put time and thought into drawing up some specific proposals to forward to Washington, and on September 16, 1880, he submitted these suggestions to Hardy's scrutiny. Hardy replied with further recommendations. And now — ten years later — Congress had acted. One cannot refrain from noticing that, among the great Victorian novelists, Hardy was almost alone in having survived to reap the harvest. Thackeray had died in 1863 and Dickens in 1870. Charles James Lever had died in 1872, the year of Hardy's *Under the Greenwood Tree*. Bulwer-Lytton died in 1873, the year of *A Pair of Blue Eyes*. Charles Kingsley died in 1875, in the time of *Ethelberta*. George Eliot's death came in 1880, the year of *The Trumpet-Major*. Trollope died in 1882 and William Harrison Ainsworth in the same year. Charles Reade died in 1884 and Wilkie Collins in 1889. This makes ten of Hardy's colleagues, all of whom might well have been glad to have James R. Osgood come along with the good news that, from now on, their books would enjoy copyright protection in America. But Hardy alone survived to hear this news. It is a strange

## LETTER NO. 6

37 Wimpole Street,[1] [London] W.
Tuesday [December 9, 1890].

My dearest Em :

Here I am — and as it wants a few minutes to breakfast I write a line to let you know. I thought of leaving Wednesday — but Mrs. Jeune says I am to stay till Thursday morning to dine with some people who are to be here Wednesday evening.

Mr. Goschen the Chancellor of the Exchequer is the only other lodger Mrs. Jeune has at present. I am to meet him at breakfast. I have told her about the knee — and she has recommended a specialist, in case it should get worse.

Yours ever
Tom.

[Postscript, written from the] Savile Club : noon.

I breakfasted with Mr. Goschen etc. — and talking about agreement stamps he and Mr. Jeune gave me some information.

The *Athenaeum* for this week contains a ballad by

comment on the habitual bent of his mind that only four years later he could write (in *Jude the Obscure*) : 'Somebody might have come along that way who might have cheered him. . . . But nobody did come, because nobody does.' Yet Osgood *had* come along. Nor does Hardy's good fortune end there. He had begun to write *Tess of the D'Urbervilles* as far back as 1888, and plans were all made for its publication in 1889 by Tillotson & Son, of Bolton. W. F. Tillotson raised objections when he discovered that Tess's story was a story of seduction, and Hardy's contract for this novel was eventually cancelled. The delay in finding a publisher now proved fortunate. The American law went into effect on July 1, 1891 ; Harper & Brothers began the serialization of *Tess* on July 18. 'How fortunate', indeed !

[1] At this date, 37 Wimpole Street was the address of Judge-Advocate and Mrs. Jeune. The Barretts had lived at No. 50 ; the Hallams at No. 67, in this same street.

Rudyard Kipling on Besant, Black, and myself, *apropos* of our letter about Harper.[1]

I will send a copy if possible. Balestier pursues me with telegrams.[2]

You can send on Wednesday's letters if they should be about anything which I can best attend to here — but if not it is unnecessary.

T.

### LETTER NO. 7

Savile Club, 107, Piccadilly, W.
Wednesday evening [December 10, 1890].

My dearest Emmie,

I think of returning to-morrow — probably by the usual 6.13 [train] — unless the fog absolutely prevents my getting out of London, or out of the house. It is dense as a wall and black as soot to-night. Luckily I have only to

[1] The lack of international-copyright protection had led the Harpers, in the summer of 1890, to issue (without Kipling's knowledge) an edition of *The Courting of Dinah Shadd and Other Stories* — stories for which the New York firm had already paid Kipling. When he learned of this publication, he sent an irate statement to the London *Athenaeum* (October 4, 1890), in which he denounced the Harpers for insulting and robbing him. On November 1 the *Athenaeum* printed 'A Reply' from Harper & Brothers. Kipling wrote 'A Counter Reply' which appeared a week later. Then, on November 22, the *Athenaeum* printed a statement signed by William Black, Walter Besant, and Thomas Hardy, in which they announced that to them it seemed 'a clear duty . . . to record the fact in the course of many years' friendly business relations with Messrs. Harper and Brothers we have always found them . . . just and liberal. . . .' This letter made Kipling more angry than ever. He dashed off an allegorical poem entitled 'The Rhyme of the Three Captains' — the 'ballad' to which Hardy here refers. Of the three 'captains', 'one was Lord of the Wessex coast'. The poem appeared in the *Athenaeum* for December 6. Kipling later included it in his Collected Verse, where readers have often been puzzled by the explanatory note prefixed to the poem. This note states that the poem 'appears to refer to one of the exploits of the notorious Paul Jones, an American pirate. It is founded on fact.'

[2] Wolcott Balestier was an American literary agent whose sister Caroline became Kipling's wife in 1892.

get from here up to Mrs. Jeune's — which is easy. She has a large dinner party to-night at 8 : but how the people will get to her I can't see at present. She is very kind and nice, and says that if you have to come to town about the lameness [in your knee] you are to stay with her. She has been to Bethnal Green this morning and I don't know where besides — although she had a large party last night (I not present) and this one to-night. She says that when you are strong, like her, it is really not so much to do as it seems. She says she wasted a shilling this morning by taking a cab, usually going in penny omnibuses.

It is like being at Portsmouths' *exactly*. Margaret's future husband is *very rich* : fancy her humour about the four chairs etc. Vernon Watney is descended from the head of the large brewing firm of that name.

I got your letter this morning : Mrs. Jeune enquires about you every day.

Ever your affectionate husband,

TOM

[P.S. :] If fog makes travelling dangerous I shall not come perhaps.

* * *

[Hardy returned to Dorchester, but six weeks later he was back again in London and again under the hospitable roof of the Jeunes.]

## LETTER NO. 8

Savile Club, 107, Piccadilly, W.

Saturday [January 24, 1891] ¼ to 5.

My dearest Em :

I telegraphed at lunch time to tell you I was not coming till Monday : and I hope you have received the message — otherwise you may be alarmed. This morning at breakfast Mrs. and Mr. Jeune both pressed me to stay over to-morrow — Irving and Ellen Terry are coming to dine with them to-morrow : and I felt I might as well stay on. I intend to return Monday, either by the 6.13, or an earlier one — probably however the first-mentioned. It rains in torrents here — and the difficulty of getting about without becoming damp is great. To-night is the first night of a comedy [1] at the *Globe* — and I am going with the rest — or rather [am] to meet them there, for I think of dining here [at the Club].

[Postscript added the next day :] I have been feeling anxious about your adventures — and wonder if it rained with you last night as it did here : if so it must have been unpleasant getting to Pearce Edgcumbe's.[2] I hope your cold is better : the air is much softer now — so that probably you have escaped a very bad cold. I called at Miss Grylls's — the gown was sent off Wednesday night — so I paid the bill. She hopes to do more for you, and to have more time and opportunity of getting your pattern. She seems anxious to go on with you. I have seen the usual men here to-day. Gosse has been attacked in last night's [3] *Pall Mall* — as you may have seen. Mrs. Jeune seems to wish we lived in town. It was a great pleasure to take the children [to the theatre] last night — or rather to be taken by them. Miss Maude Stanley also accompanied us — (the two girls, she and I altogether [*sic*]) and

[1] 'All the Comforts of Home', an adaptation by W. Gillette and H. Duckworth of a German farce.

[2] Robert Pearce-Edgcumbe was Mayor of Dorchester in 1891. He lived at Somerleigh Court, Dorchester, to which address Hardy had (on August 8, 1890) taken Alfred Parsons, the painter, to see some paintings by Sir Joshua Reynolds. Pearce-Edgcumbe was knighted in 1895.

[3] This appears to be a slip on Hardy's part for 'last week's', for it was in the issue of the *Pall Mall Budget* for January 15, 1891 (page 21) that the 'attack' occurred : 'Mr. Edmund Gosse . . . thinks that English Poetry . . . is not so much liked now as it was a few years ago. . . . Surely this is far from the actual state of the case. . . .'

as she said, it is not always one gets taken to theatres by such experienced playgoers. Their eyes were so bright and their whisperings incessant, in their anxiety that we should not miss the points of the performance. Mrs. Jeune would have gone, but had to attend a Conservative ball (quite a mixed affair) and could not.

The rain still pours down — and I have to get back to Wimpole Street (first calling at a shirt-makers for an extra shirt if I can). I have declined to dine with them to-night — not anticipating such weather.

If you have time to write a line to-morrow, will you mention the number of the house Lady Margaret is going to in Berkeley Square : (if she mentions it in her letter) Mrs. Jeune wants to know. Direct to 37 Wimpole St.

The Jeune's are leaving — yes — really — at Easter — and going [to move] into Harley Street — exactly at the back of [their] present house.

Ever yours
Tom.

## LETTER NO. 9

Savile Club, 107, Piccadilly. W.
Saturday [April 11, 1891].

My dearest Em :

I have received your letter. Nothing has happened here, except that I have called on Osgood : the book is coming out about the first week in May.[1] The weather is so bad here — a cold east wind, with now and then a drizzle, that I am glad you are not in town for your own sake, though not for mine, everything being so dull. A certain lack of energy I feel may be owing to having hitherto kept to milk and water as a beverage in alternative to tea. I went to the Gaiety theatre last night — some of the

[1] *A Group of Noble Dames* was, in the final event, published by Osgood, McIlvaine & Co. on May 30, 1891.

14

burlesque was funny — some of it stupid. 'The bogie
man' which I went to hear, is not much. 'That's how you
mesmerize him,' another song in the piece, is funnier. I
have written two pages of MS. and shall recover energy
no doubt next week. I am at the *annexe* of the [West
Central] hotel [in Southampton Row] — a comfortable
room — except that the street is noisy at night — all the
single rooms are in front. I am going to try Mr Herriot's
plan of wool in the ears to-night. I have slept however
pretty well — and have no dyspepsia at all. I lunched
with Besant yesterday here [at the Club] : we met by
accident. I should not go to the 'at home,' unless you
wish to. Next week I shall look about more [for a flat
or other lodgings] and write again.

Ever your affectionate husband<br>Tom.

## LETTER NO. 10

Savile Club, 107, Piccadilly. W.<br>Monday [April 13, 1891] 5 p.m.

My dearest Em :
I have just come from calling on Besant at the Office
of the Society of Authors, where he is now acting as
secretary in the absence of the regular man. He seems to
delight in it, and gloats over the villainies of publishers
that he unearths from day to day.

I received your letter and enclosures this morning —
and posted the corrections back to [J. Addington] Symonds
— anything of value it will be safest to send here — but
if imperative that I should get it quite early in the morning
the hotel will do. I will let you know if I move into
lodgings. One thing I find is that Bloomsbury is too far
from the Club etc. — I am continually in omnibuses —
and we must get nearer. I wish Chapel Place were still

available. I will inquire about the flat if I can. Have you yet heard of the death of Colonel Hambro of Milton Abbey, the member [of Parliament] for South Dorset? He died Saturday at Monte Carlo.[1] Now there will have to be a bye-election — and I suppose Pearce Edgecumbe will stand. I hear that as Hambro's death was so sudden (though he had been ailing), the Unionists have nobody ready to fill his place. I wonder if the fact of Pearce Edgecumbe being Mayor will prevent his standing?

Yesterday it was very wet in the afternoon, but I went to Gosse's to meet Mme Darmsteter.[2] She looks rather more matronly than formerly — though one rather wonders what reason there is for her doing so, her husband being so small. I talked to him, and like him much : he is very warm and genial — and would like us to come and see them in Paris.

The weather is not quite so bad to-day — but I have very little zest for London, and cannot get up any interest in theatres or other entertainments. You must decide for yourself about coming. I have been writing here all morning — that sketch for the *Fortnightly* [3] — and lunched with Kipling.

Your affectionate husband
Tom.

[1] Charles J. T. Hambro died on April 11, 1891, at the age of fifty-five.
[2] Agnes Mary Francis Robinson, born 1857, had married (in 1888) James Darmesteter, Professor of Iranian languages and literature at the Collège de France. Hardy misspelled his name.
[3] The *Fortnightly* for May 1891 carried Hardy's, 'The Midnight Baptism' — salvaged from a chapter in *Tess of the D'Urbervilles* which he had had to discard in order to render the novel acceptable for serialization in the *Graphic*. This 'sketch' thus became the first part of *Tess* to achieve publication. Osgood's three-volume edition of *Tess* did not appear until November.

## LETTER NO. 11

Savile Club, 107, Piccadilly. W.
Thursday [April 16, 1891].

My dearest Em :

I return the dividend warrants signed — and please pay them in to the Bank with the other things. Your letter was marked *Tuesday* morning : but I did not get it till to-day. I sent the MS. of The Midnight Baptism (as I [finally] called it) [1] to the *Fortnightly Review* and they are going to send proof at once. I just *glanced* at lodgings yesterday — but was too overpowered to do anything in the matter till you come. I am hastening away from the Club again, so write in a hurry. I think we must settle down in a quiet lodging, where I can work, for I am quite indifferent to society at present : and even engrossed in the matter of a story which shall have its scene in London — I am going out looking about on that account now.

Will you ask the gardener before you come when and how he wishes to be paid ? I think we might make Polly Antell our agent for paying him. There are envelopes of all sizes in the third drawer down of the chest in the study. Let me have a note to the hotel address on the morning of the day you will arrive — communications with any important enclosure send here [to the Club] for safety.

Your ever affectionate husband

Tom.

## LETTER NO. 12

Savile Club, 107, Piccadilly. W.
Saturday [April 18, 1891].

My dearest Em :

I received your letter this morning — after a night of slight headache. I am not very vigorous yet — and care

[1] He had at first proposed to call it 'The Bastard's Baptism'.

most to get some lodgings not very central and read a
good deal. I have not received proofs from [the] *Fortnightly Review* — so I suppose the story will not appear
next month.[1] If they have been sent to Dorchester forward them here at once. Gosse has asked me to go to a
morning performance of *Hedda Gabler* (Ibsen's play which
he has translated) on Monday [April 20 at] 2.30 [at the
Vaudeville Theatre] — and I accepted — forgetting that
you might be arriving at that very moment. If so, however, it will not matter much, as I will leave word at the
Hotel that you are to be expected. I find I am getting too
old [2] to turn out of a morning and *go* [*out*] to work — so
we must get a comfortable sitting room.[3] Haggard is
back from Mexico [4] — I have just been talking to him.
Yesterday lunched with Kipling and his father. I have had
some tea, and the headache has gone off somewhat.

Your affectionate husband<br>Tom.

## LETTER NO. 13

Savile Club, 107, Piccadilly. W.<br>Tuesday [April 5, 1892].

My dearest Em,
    I am staying over to-night at Lady Jeune's — she
having a dinner-party at which she wants me to be present.
Meanwhile I have looked a little for lodgings and have
found a comfortable place not far from the Jeunes, and near
Mme Tussaud's [Wax Works] — in Beaumont Street (see
map) — which I think may do — for a week at any rate.

---

[1] But it did !    [2] Hardy was now fifty.
[3] They eventually rented a flat in Mandeville Place.
[4] Unusual interest attaches to this bit of information, for the visit of
H. Rider Haggard to Mexico is not mentioned in the *D.N.B.* (1932) or in
*Who's Who* (1925) or in the *Encyclopaedia Britannica* (1929). Haggard
visited Mexico in the company of J. G. Jebb, to whom he dedicated his
novel, *Montezuma's Daughter*, in 1893.

What I suggest is that you come up Thursday morning — and I will meet you. I have not taken the place — but even if it should be gone I can get another as I find lodgings are not so difficult to get as in some seasons.

Lady Jeune seems to wish us to be not so far off as South Kensington. She is going away from the 3d June for six weeks and would like us to call upon the children, if we are in town.

Anyhow come up to please yourself as to time — and I will meet you if you let me know. Even if I take lodgings for a week, and you change your mind about date, the payment will not be ruinous — and I must have a place somewhere.

I feel rather tired. The Jeunes are very nice. She says the Sheridans [from Wool, Dorset] were at her crush last Saturday night.

Yours affectionately<br>TOM.

## LETTER NO. 14

Athenaeum Club, Pall Mall, S.W.[1]<br>Monday [May 23, 1892] – 9 p.m.

My dearest Em :

We buried Osgood this afternoon.[2] When we were in the [Kensall Green] cemetery chapel and the officiating minister was reading the words 'O death, where is thy sting,' etc. I looked at my watch, and it was exactly half past 4.[3] Osgood had no relative in England : [his partner, Clarence W.] McIlvaine and [William M.] Laffan (an

[1] Hardy had been elected a member in April 1891.

[2] James Ripley Osgood died on May 20, 1892, at the age of fifty-six. See Letter No. 5, footnote 1.

[3] Hardy here illustrates his possession of a characteristic which he had ascribed to his hero Egbert Mayne (in *An Indiscretion in the Life of an Heiress*): 'The day and the minute . . . became registered in his mind with the indelibility of ink. Years afterwards he could recall at a moment's notice . . . that on the ninth it rained at a quarter past two . . . that on the seventeenth the grass was rather too wet for a lady's feet ; and other calendrical and meteorological facts of no value whatever either to science or history.'

American friend, who happened to be in London) walked as Chief Mourners, and [William] Black and myself next — behind us came Abbey,[1] Boughton,[2] [George] du Maurier,[3] etc. The grave was in wet clay — and before we left it was more than half filled in.[4] Very sad.

I have only been to Lady Jeune's to leave my things, as she is dining out. To-morrow I will look for lodgings. I will, if possible, write again in time for you to get the letter Wednesday morning — as of course I cannot suggest anything as yet. If you *wish* to come Wednesday no doubt I shall have some place by that time — or a place at the West Central Hotel, or some other.

I do not propose to stay at Lady Jeune's longer than over to-morrow night, at longest.

Yours affectionately,<br>
TOM.

## LETTER NO. 15

Athenaeum Club, Pall Mall S.W.<br>
Thursday afternoon [? May 26, 1892 ?].

My dearest Em :

Will you let me know if [the investment brokers] Foster & Braithwaite have sent a letter acknowledging the

[1] In view of the curious fact that Edwin Austin Abbey (1852–1911) is not mentioned in either *The Early Life* or *The Later Years of Thomas Hardy* it may be well to state here that this American painter was sent to England by Harper & Brothers in 1878, that he became a member of the Savile Club, where he knew Hardy, and that the two exchanged invitations over a period of many years. On June 21, 1886, for example, Mrs. Hardy invited Abbey to tea at 28 Upper Bedford Place, Russell Square.

[2] George Henry Boughton had provided illustrations for some of the books published by Osgood.

[3] du Maurier had illustrated two of the Wessex novels : *The Hand of Ethelberta* and *A Laodicean*.

[4] Later on, when money was being collected to place a marker on the grave, Hardy, 'with much pleasure', sent a cheque 'as a slight expression of my wish to be included among those who propose to erect a stone to the memory of Mr. Osgood'.

receipt of a cheque I sent from here to them last Tuesday. Also will you ask Emily [? house-keeper] if Matthews [the gardener at Max Gate] has been regular since Monday. He was not there when I left [? to attend Osgood's funeral]. Find out how many days he has been [there], and pay him Saturday evening at the rate of 2/6 a day.

I return Monday, so far as I know.

Yours affectionately,

T.

## LETTER NO. 16

Athenaeum Club, Pall Mall, S.W.
Wednesday afternoon [October 12, 1892].

My dearest Em :

I have attended Tennyson's funeral — and find I cannot get back very well to-night — so I will wait till to-morrow — returning about the usual time — though possibly by the Salisbury train, about twenty minutes later than the 6.13.

Owing to some slight confusion in the [funeral] arrangements many people who should have been in the procession were not, but were standing elsewhere. I had a very good place [in the Abbey] — and looked into the grave [in Poets' Corner] with the rest as we passed it on our way out.

George Meredith was there — also Henry James, Huxley, etc. I will tell you more when I come.

Yours always,

TOM.

## LETTER NO. 17

79, Harley Street, [London] W.[1]
Monday, July 24 [1893].[2]

My dear Em : [3]

I have received this morning your letter and the en-closures. Any book parcels that come are sent by me as purchased, not to have the trouble of bringing them.

I am very tired and am doing next to nothing. If I had not promised Sir. H. Thompson to dine with him Wednesday I should have returned [home] this morning. London is dreary and oppressive. Lady Jeune had a small dinner party last night — and we went to the Irving farewell performance Saturday night. But, curiously enough, my reluctance to meet the Duchess of Teck at Mrs. Kennard's, on the [first] anniversary, too, of father's death,[4] had something prophetic in it. A few hours before the dinner the Duke's sister died, he had to go off to Ger-many, and the Duchess, of course, could not dine [out]. After all, the meeting, if ever it takes place, will be where I wished it to be, at Lady Jeune's.

My fellow lodger the first day was Prince Victor Albert, Princess Christian's son — and since then it has been Lady Bantry, a widowed young Countess whose history is rather pathetic. I will tell you about her.

Lady Jeune and all of them are extremely kind. A

---

[1] The new address of Sir Francis and Lady Jeune.

[2] Two months before this date, Hardy and his wife had paid a Whit-suntide visit to Ireland. From May 19 to 25 they stayed at the Vice-regal Lodge in Dublin as the guests of Mrs. Arthur Henniker (*née* Florence E. H. Milnes, daughter of the first Lord Houghton). She was acting as hostess for her brother, the second Lord Houghton, who was then Lord Lieutenant of Ireland. There are some students of Hardy who profess to notice an increase in the tensions at Max Gate after the date of this Irish visit.

[3] The reader may note in passing that this is the first time that Hardy writes 'dear' instead of 'dearest'.

[4] Hardy's father died on July 20, 1892, at the age of eighty-one.

slight gloom has been thrown over the household by the doctor, who after seeing Sir Francis, has peremptorily ordered him to Royant [*sic*], to take the waters, a place under the Puy de Dome, central France. He was going to Scotland for his holiday, and elsewhere : and as Lady Jeune cannot accompany him abroad, will have to spend it in making a cure in banishment. I will let you know time of my arrival.

Yours affectionately,

\*   \*   \*                              T.

[Since, of Hardy's letters to Emma, this is the only one dated 1893, we are left wondering why. Did he write her no other in this year, or did she destroy what he wrote ? In conjecturing how best to explain the gap in the correspondence, we are forced to turn to other sources of information about the year 1893. When Sarah Grand's *The Heavenly Twins* appeared, Charles J. Hankinson took Madame Grand to call on the Hardys at Max Gate.

Mrs. Hardy expressed warm approval of this book, while Hardy looked on with a sardonic smile. At the lunch table the conversation drifted on to general philosophical views of life. Hardy stated his abhorrence of pious pretensions which have no counterpart in conduct. Mrs. Hardy was shocked ; Madame Grand was amused. The next morning Hankinson received a note from Mrs. Hardy, saying that she hoped he would not take any of Mr. Hardy's remarks seriously ; that he really didn't mean them ; that he was a very religious man who read his Greek Testament regularly, and that his religious beliefs were in reality quite orthodox. Mr. Hankinson records having similar notes from Max Gate 'on several other occasions'. (*Hardy of Wessex*, by Carl J. Weber, page 164.)

T. P. O'Connor gives a similar report of Mrs. Hardy's conduct. He recalled how, after he had entertained the Hardys at dinner, Mrs. Hardy returned the following day to talk about her husband. O'Connor quotes as her words : 'You know, he's very vain and very selfish. And these women that he meets in

London society only increase these things. They are the poison;
I am the antidote.' To O'Connor her purpose seemed to be to
belittle, irritate, and discourage her husband. Purdy states that
'Mrs. Hardy's growing eccentricities were painfully manifest'
at the time of the May visit to Dublin. As for Hardy himself,
books and letters survive which free us to some extent from
vague conjecture. We know that upon his return from
Ireland, he and Mrs. Henniker began a vigorous correspondence ; and when she shortly followed him back to England,
there were frequent meetings. In June he gave her a copy of
*Tess* ; in July, a copy of *A Laodicean* ; in September, a copy
of *Desperate Remedies*. In October they began to collaborate
in writing a gruesome story called 'The Spectre of the Real',
and this collaboration involved further frequent meetings. In
his poem 'The Coming of the End' he speaks of 'That journey
of one day a week', and another of his poems — one that John
Middleton Murry has called 'one of the finest of modern
lyrical poems' : 'A Broken Appointment' — is probably addressed to her (although her name does not appear). In this
poem Hardy calls himself 'a time-torn man'. In all, there are
at least a dozen poems which can be plausibly related to Mrs.
Henniker. In 1893 she was thirty-eight ; Hardy was fifty-
three. In January 1904 he gave her a copy of the first part of
*The Dynasts* ; in February 1906, a copy of Part Two ; and in
February 1908, a copy of the last part. The friendship gradually tapered off (it 'stopped without a jerk', according to one
of his poems), and the evidence in his verses supports the conclusion that his interest in her was warmer than hers in him ;
also, that the friendship never went beyond the bounds of
friendship, even when the two met (for example) at an inn
in Winchester. Emma Hardy doubtless had good reason for
thinking that her husband's conduct at this time indicated a
change in his attitude towards his wife, but (as Rebekah Owen
expressed it long afterwards, after knowing both husband and
wife for twenty years) 'I believe his fidelity to her to have been

*perfect'*. That may have been true in a legal sense, but there can be little doubt about the fact that Hardy's emotions in 1893 strayed from Max Gate. When Mrs. Gertrude Atherton arrived from California and met Hardy on various occasions in London, 'in his wake was an excessively plain, dowdy, high-stomached woman with her hair drawn back in a tight little knot.' It was Mrs. Hardy, and Mrs. Atherton jumped to the conclusion that 'no doubt Hardy went out so constantly to be rid of her'. Some years before this, Hardy had written in his notebook : 'Love lives on propinquity, but dies of contact'.]

## LETTER NO. 18

79 Harley St. [London]
Saturday [March 31, 1894] — 1 p.m.

My dear Em :
    The day goes so quickly that I have hardly time to write a line. I am now going on to lunch at Lady London-derry's — and this evening I take Lady Jeune's girls to the theatre. They are such dears that it is a pleasure to go with them. The political excitement at Gladstone's resignation out-vies everything just now. *The Speaker* to-day [IX : 367] quotes one of the candid sentences from *Life's Little Ironies* and adds — (*apropos* of women's novels, like *Keynotes*, etc.) 'so that the old hands know a thing or two as well as the young 'uns.' Do not send on press cuttings — or anything after Monday night.
    The Duchess of Manchester is away at Pau for her health.
    I fear I shall not have time to see about [renting] a house. I am rather tired already. I shall have to come up again about it — or you must, as you did last year. I don't much mind not going to H. Terrace.

Yours affectionately,
T.

## LETTER NO. 19

79 Harley St.
Sunday [April 1, 1894].

My dearest Em :

I am not coming Tuesday after all. Lady Jeune has a dinner, and big party afterwards, on Wednesday, for which she has asked me to stay, and I have decided to do so : so that I shall arrive some time *Thursday* — probably by the 6.13. It is rather a sudden party, to meet the Princess Mary — and they have sent out 500 invitations — so that the squash will be pretty fierce, and I shall be glad to be on the *inside* all the time.

I took the [Jeune] girls to the theatre last night — and was more amused by their innocent talk than by the play — though they give me some laughable specimens of slang. 'I do hope it will be something very *risqué*,' said Dorothy. 'So as to make our hair curl !' the point of it being that they would turn round and ask me *if it was risqué* — not knowing of their own judgment.

I lunched (did I tell you ?) with Lady Londonderry Saturday, and met the Lord Chancellor, and others. He is, as you know, a son-in-law of Mr. Kindersley's, of Clyffe. Today at Lady Jeune's Lord Randolph Churchill lunched — also T. P. O'Connor and Mrs. T. P., Lord Morris (Judge of Appeal), etc. etc. Unfortunately I can't do a line of writing. Lady Jeune thinks you ought to see an oculist, and wear carefully chosen spectacles (we were talking of sight — that's how it came out [that you have been having trouble with your eyes]). Whatever has been extracted from the article in *The Young Man* for the *Dorset County Chronicle* has been done by the Editor — nobody would send it, of course.

Post on letters (not cuttings or papers) therefore, up to Wednesday night. Yours affectionately,

Tom.

[P.S. :] In addition to the above-named I have met Lady Hilda Broderick, Sir E. Lawson (proprietor of *Daily Telegraph*), Buckle (*Times*), Lady Dorothy Nevill (whose last words were 'Be sure you let me know when Mrs. Hardy comes.'), Hon. George Curzon, Sir Redvers Buller, [and] Sir F. Lockwood.

## LETTER NO. 20

Savile Club, Piccadilly, W.
Tuesday [April 3, 1894].

My dearest Em :

Nothing has happened since Sunday worth reporting — except, perhaps, my lunching with Lady Pembroke [1] — which was yesterday. She is much older than her husband — and a woman I rather like — she says I am to let her know when we both come to town to stay. To meet me were Lord Rowton [2], two ladies with titles whose names I just now forget — and Mrs. Lyttleton, whom we met in Dublin [last May] — a thin, rather good-looking woman — her husband Colonel Lyttleton is one of the officials there, I think — and is a nephew of Mr. or Mrs. Gladstone.

I had a nod from John Morley yesterday — which was as much, certainly, as I wanted, for it was just when he was rushing off to the Cabinet meeting, and I tried to avoid him, knowing how such men are bored at such times.

Lady Morris has sent me a card for her party Thursday night — but I have written to say I shan't come.

If Matthews calls tell him he can dig some ground and

[1] She was one of the descendants of Betty, 'First Countess of Wessex' about whom Hardy had written in *A Group of Noble Dames*. Hardy liked to inform people that he knew eight of her descendants.

[2] Another descendant of the First Countess of Wessex. Lord Ilchester had expressed vehement disapproval of Hardy's taking liberty with family-history in his story. Lord Rowton remarked to Hardy : 'It's all nonsense, you know, of Ilchester to feel so, and I shall tell him so'.

put in *parsnips* and broad beans — same as last year. Will
*you* send for the seed — to Harris's.

I am trying to get to Kensington to look at or enquire
for a house.

Ever affectionately

T.

[P.S. :] I lunch with George Curzon Thursday — so that
I shall not get home till the 8.27 train.


## LETTER NO. 21

Savile Club, 107, Piccadilly, W.

Wednesday [? April 3, 1895 ?].

My dearest Em :

I arrived safely : and went to see Lord Pembroke
almost immediately, since, though I was on my way to
look at the houses, I found it was just the time of afternoon
that he had mentioned. I had a very pleasant time there
(the Doctor's house he is in is just at the back of this Club).
— He looked so handsome as he lay in bed in his coloured
shirt — and he was in good spirits. When Lady Pembroke
came in afterwards he said he was almost well. Mrs.
Lyttleton was sitting there with him — she has been in
London for some time.

I have looked at the houses and flats. I still think 16
Pelham Crescent suits us best. It is, too, near the South
Kensington Museum which is an instructive place to
wander in.

I was going to look at some more this afternoon, but
I feel tired.

I have also called at Osgood McIlvaine & Co.[1]

---

[1] Behind this apparently simple sentence there lies an immense amount
of personal and literary history. In December 1890 (see Letter No. 5)

*Letter No. 22*

I suppose I shall return tomorrow afternoon.

Yours very affectionately

Том.

## LETTER NO. 22

79 Harley Street, W.
Monday [? April 8, 1895 ?].

My dear Em,
I am absolutely undecided about what to do, at present.
I did think of writing and suggesting that you should meet

Hardy had discussed with James R. Osgood the publication of a collected edition of his works. He eventually signed a contract with Osgood for the issuance of such a series, and while this was in preparation, Osgood's firm published various Hardy titles (see Letter 9 and Letter 10, footnote 3). Osgood died in 1892 (see Letter 14), but the collected edition for which he had contracted with Hardy began to appear on schedule in 1895 — Osgood's partner, Clarence McIlvaine, carrying out the plan for the publication of sixteen volumes at monthly intervals. *Tess* appeared April 4, 1895 ; *Far from the Madding Crowd*, in May ; *The Mayor*, in June ; etc. Hardy's mention of 'neglected proofs' (see Letter 23) refers to this collected edtioni. When *Jude the Obscure* appeared on November 1 of this year, its publication passed without notice in Hardy's letters to his wife ; but this silence will not mislead the reader whose ears have been kept open to reports from other sources. Mrs. Hardy talked to her physician (Dr. Fred B. Fisher) about *Jude the Obscure.* When she found out what Hardy was putting into this story (for example, Sue's remarks about 'how hopelessly vulgar an institution legal marriage is'), Mrs. Hardy threw the pages away from her in disgust and told Dr. Fisher that 'she'd never have anything more to do with any book her husband wrote'. She never did. But she did not stop there. She wrote to Dr. Richard Garnett at the British Museum and asked his help in trying to persuade Hardy to suppress his 'vicious' manuscript. When her letter proved unavailing, she made a special trip to London, and repeated her request to Garnett. She implored him ; she wept. The young Garnetts, on hearing of this episode, were either appalled or amused, depending upon their age and individual leanings. But between horrified gasps and amused snickers, the news got around in the British Museum (and eventually, of course, into the world outside) that Mrs. Hardy had been trying to prevent the publication of her husband's novel.

In all fairness to Emma Hardy, it ought to be added that she was by no means alone in her dislike of *Jude the Obscure.* The Bishop of Wakefield threw the book in the fire. A lecturer at Liverpool spoke of its 'filth and defilement'. Jeannette L. Gilder wrote a scandalized review in the New

me at Brighton for a few days, as the Jeunes say it will be by far the best seaside place both for me and for you — and Lady Jeune has given me the address of a place we can go to. But this can be put off, and I am inclined to come home Wednesday. Brighton is such a distance for you to go to for a few days : and as Ada does not go till the 19th you would have to get back again so soon. Moreover Easter [April 14, 1895] comes next week, and I don't think I should care much to be at Brighton then.

However I will do just which you like.

I feel absolutely unable to do anything here, unless I am in a place of my own. It turns out that you are quite right about a flat with attendance. I saw Oswald Crawfurd yesterday, and both he and Lady Jeune say that will be the thing for us. The Crawfurds live like that permanently at Queen Anne's Mansions — and he says that Mrs. Lynn Linton wants to let hers. No servant at all required. Shall I communicate with her about it ? We should not want one till after Easter.        Yours affectionately,

Том.

York *World* in which she denounced the 'immorality' in *Jude* and 'its coarseness which is beyond belief'.

Hardy's forbearance, in these letters of 1895, is all the more remarkable when these facts are kept in mind ; but his silence ought not to be mis-interpreted, as it has been in one recent study (*Thomas Hardy*, by Douglas Brown, London, 1961) in which the reader is told (p. 19) that in 1895 Hardy 'and Emma experienced a brief return of happiness', and (p. 99) that 'much of his wife went into the . . . study of Sue' in *Jude the Obscure*. Nothing could be farther from the truth ! At this time Hardy was composing his three poems entitled 'In Tenebris' (published in 1902). In the first he remarks that

> 'love can not make smart
> Again this year his heart
> Who no heart hath.'

In the second he thinks of himself as 'one born out of due time' who 'dis-turbs the order here'. And in the third he records having learned 'that the world was a welter of futile doing'. In 1895 there was no 'brief return of happiness' for Thomas Hardy. These letters of that year are eloquent by what they do *not* say.

[P.S. :] If you wish for Brighton, it would be best to go, say Wednesday. I could meet you at Waterloo [Station] and go on the same day.

## LETTER NO. 23

Athenaeum Club Pall Mall
Wednesday [April 24, 1895] 1.0 p.m.

My dearest Em :

I wired to you just now to say that I had taken a place at last — 90 Ashley Gardens [Westminster]. It was the best thing I could do, I thought. We could not have 16 Pelham Crescent, Mrs. Fyler being too unwell to leave for a fortnight. My choice lay between the Flat taken and a delightful house between Hyde Park Gardens and Sussex Gardens, on the north side of the Park. Had it not been for getting to the Athenaeum Club, I should have taken the house, which was beautifully furnished. But I thought convenience above everything, and Ashley Gardens being nearer Victoria Station you will be able to get to your Club by a Royal Blue [bus] easily — and we shall be *close* to the Army & Navy Stores — near the Abbey, etc. — as you will see if you look at the map. I have not yet seen what kind of china etc. they have at the Flat. If you write a list of a few things I must look for it will help you perhaps to know what to bring up.

They don't leave their servants behind, so you must bring a parlour maid. As we enter Tuesday I do not see any use in your coming till then. Do you think I need come home to come up with you ? I hardly see the necessity — and I am overwhelmed with neglected proofs which I want to get at.[1]

[1] Osgood, McIlvaine & Co. had begun issuing the collected uniform edition of Hardy's works, in 16 volumes, 1895–1896.

What I should require you to bring for me would be my big portmanteau and in it all the things on the enclosed list. I may write again to-day, or at any moment, as things come into my head. I do not *think* any rugs are necessary — but I will look, and let you know.

One advantage of the Flat is that Mrs. Patrick Campbell lives in an adjoining block — and if the play [1] goes on that may be convenient for the work.

There is a nice entrance-hall to the Flat — I mean our own flat — *inside* our door on the landing.

Ever yours
Tom.

[P.S. :] Will you tell Henry when he is to begin paying John etc. Also leave say 10/- with John for paying little charges.


LETTER NO. 24

The Athenaeum Pall Mall. S.W.
Friday [April 26, 1895].

My dear Em :

I feel better to-day — and do not think of coming back — till, at any rate, you are here. I sat here resting all yesterday afternoon, and went to bed at a little past 8.

If no *trouble*, will you bring the little bottle of almond oil from the dressing table in the small bedroom. But if there is any danger of your breaking it, don't bring it — as it would only save 6d. and the oil would ruin everything.

The best plan will be to send by goods train the packing cases etc. so as not to be encumbered.

It would save trouble, I should think, if you and the

---

[1] Hardy's own dramatization of his novel, *Tess of the D'Urbervilles*. In the final outcome, the play did *not* 'go on', and Mrs. Campbell was disappointed. Hardy had to wait until 1924 before his play was finally produced.

servants come by the same train — but not same class. 10.29 Southwestern Railway would be best. I can meet you at station, but perhaps it would be best if I were at the flat to receive you.

Tell John to hang up a sheet of brown paper in the new attic window — as the sun blazes in hot — and to guard against sun generally.

It has been very warm here. I have met at this Club two of Her Majesty's ministers, John Morley, and Acland — also Lord de Tabley (who is coming to see us). Mrs. Henniker also writes to say she is coming to see you.

Ever affectionately,<br>Tom.

[P.S. :] The woman at the flat says she has a very good china tea service, but I have not seen it.

## LETTER NO. 25

The Athenaeum Pall Mall S.W.<br>Saturday [April 27, 1895]

My dear Em :

I have received your letter, post card, and the other letters. Perhaps John had better make one exception to not sending on packets open at the ends, and send Durrants' press cuttings.

You had better come to Waterloo [Station] — as it would take you much longer to come to Victoria — and you would only save 6d. cab fare.

I was afraid you might think by my advising you not to come till Tuesday that I did not want you here. Of course I do, as it is very lonely and dismal [here without you] — I meant solely on your own account. If you don't mind the wear and tear of changing lodgings etc. — you might come Monday to the Alexandra Club. But be sure you don't start till you have *secured* the bedroom by telegraph — and had a *reply* — as every place is *crammed*. At the hotel I am up in a miserable attic, nearly suffocated, and they are turning away scores of people every day.

I may write again, if there is anything to say.

Ever affectionately,

Toм.

## LETTER NO. 26

The Athenaeum, Pall Mall, S.W.
Wednesday night, July 24th [1895].

My dear Em :

I have just received your note and enclosures. George Curzon's dinner I will accept, as I am all alone, and the evenings are dismal. I will send a cheque to Barkers — and another when the other bill comes. One letter you enclosed was from Miss Shirley about the grate. There has been no rain here in the *day*time. I think I should accept the Thorntons' invitation — for both [of us] — and if I am not at home you can go alone.

I am going to meet Mr. Forbes Robertson at his house to-morrow morning about the play [1] — if all goes well I shall have to see solicitor, etc. — so that I shall be some days before anything is settled, I suppose. It is not altogether cheerful to be here now that we have no foothold — and the season seems over. I *live* almost entirely at this Club or at the Savile. I am going to see Lady Fitzgerald and [her sister] Mrs. Henniker on Friday — and will tell the latter about the neuralgic remedy. They are leaving London in a few days I think.

I *think* that before I come back [to Max Gate] I will go and stay at the Jeunes' for a day or two — if they can have

[1] Hardy's dramatization of *Tess* was still under discussion (see Letter 23, fn. on p. 32). Forbes-Robertson was to play Angel Clare to Mrs. Campbell's Tess. Nothing came of the proposal.

me. I wish we had a permanent place here — it would be so much nicer.[1] But I don't see how to afford £200 a year for [a] flat. Mr. Spencer Smith happens to be in Town *en garçon* like me — and we meet here. You will have seen that Birrell has got in — whom I know a little, that Conybeare is out — and that Sir W. Harcourt has been elected for West Monmouth after his overthrow at Derby.

I have been reading here — Max Nordau's *Conventional Lies* this afternoon. I went to the City this morning, and got the hinges for the spare room.

Ever affectionately,

TOM.

## LETTER NO. 27

The Priory, Reigate.[2]

Sunday 11 a.m. [? October 27, 1895 ?][3]

My dear Em :

I arrived here without incident — not going into London at all — further than Waterloo Station — where I simply changed into the South-eastern train — having a little lunch at the refreshment room. It has rained without ceasing ever since I left home. Mrs. Craigie arrived by the train which brought me. There are also staying here Mr Richmond Ritchie (Miss Thackeray's husband), an American literary man — Mr. Adams — another man from Oxford — another just [arrived] from China, and Lady Granby.

I shall not, I suppose, be able to get home to-morrow

[1] This sentence should be given careful attention by those misguided persons who have described Hardy as a hermit living on the fringe of Egdon Heath, with no knowledge of (or interest in) dwellers in the city.

[2] One of the 'seats' of Lady Henry Somerset, south of London on the road to Brighton.

[3] The date is uncertain. In *Later Years* (p. 37) Hardy speaks of 'a hiatus which cannot be filled'. This letter may help to fill one day of the hiatus. Regarding the silence of this autumn, see Letter 21, footnote 1.

(Monday) but if I do come I suppose it will be by the
8.30 [train].
Yours affectionately,
Tom.

## LETTER NO. 28

Savile Club, 107, Piccadilly. W.
Sunday night 2.2.96 [February 2, 1896].

My dear Em :
I arrived safely : but London is rather dreary out
of doors — easterly breeze, grey fog, not very much. I
sat an hour or two to Miss [Winifred Hope] Thomson
to-day : [1] and after lunching with her, her sister, and step-
father, Mr Fletcher Moulton, I went to see Mrs. Crackanthorpe. There I met Miss Elizabeth Robins,[2] and Violet
Hunt. Miss Robins came away with me, and we walked
together nearly to Hyde Park Corner. I then called on
the Hennikers. The Major (who is really a very good
fellow) was very amusing — describing the only time ever
he studied poetry : when he was getting engaged to
Mrs. Henniker — at which time he bought a copy of
Byron, and read him manfully through. He then got
married, and has never read any since.[3]

[1] In May 1895 Miss Thomson had begun a painted portrait of Hardy,
but had had trouble in getting the hand right. After completing the painting, she had it hung. Later, it was presented to Hardy himself, and after
his death, the second Mrs. Hardy gave it to Hardye's School, Dorchester,
where it now hangs in the Library. A photograph of this portrait was published in *Letters of Thomas Hardy* (facing page 62), edited by Carl J. Weber
(Waterville : Colby College Press, 1954).

[2] This actress, like Mrs. Patrick Campbell, was eager to appear as Tess
in a dramatization of Hardy's novel. She apparently thought that Hardy
had promised her the part and on March 18, 1896, wrote him to express
her surprise on hearing that he had 'entered into negotiations with Mrs.
Campbell'.

[3] When Major-General Arthur Henry Henniker died, February 6,
1912, Hardy wrote a poem of three quatrains in his memory. Mrs. Henniker
published this poem, 'A. H., 1855–1912', in October 1912 in a little book
of obituary reminiscences and letters. Hardy never collected it.

A ticket for Lord Leighton's funeral was sent to me here.[1] It is at 12 to-morrow.

Yours affectionately,

Tom.

## LETTER NO. 29

Savile Club, 107, Piccadilly. W.
Monday night [February 3, 1896].

My dear Em :

I have got over most of the fearful depression,[2] slight headache etc., which I had up to last night — and made me feel I could not possibly stay on [here]. I shall now probably be here till Friday, returning by the 8.30 train.

I called on Lady Jeune to-day, and she was so kind and insistent that I am going there to-morrow. It is so very *dismal* at the West Central Hotel.

Miss Thomson finished painting the hand to-day.

I went to Leighton's funeral. It was a slight fog early — but the sun broke through it, and shone into the Cathedral. The dead march was impressive — and so was the scene altogether. I saw there a good many I knew. Sir W. Besant, and John Collier[3] sat next me, and Mrs. Clifford was a little way off.

It is *very* cold, and raw, but not very foggy. I don't think you could stand it here just now. If I take a house *soon*, you must promise to come straight up into it, and not to go out of doors while this sort of weather lasts.

I have seen the loveliest 'Byke' for myself — would suit me admirably — 'The Rover Cob'. It is £20 ! I can't tell if I ought to have it.[4]

[1] Frederick Lord Leighton, P.R.A., died on January 24, 1896, at Holland Park Road, London, at the age of sixty-six.

[2] This depression no doubt contributed to the mood in which 'In Tenebris' was written. See the footnote to Letter 21.

[3] This artist had illustrated Hardy's novel *The Trumpet-Major*.

[4] Hardy was now nearly fifty-six years old. His interest in cycling increased rather than diminished.

I think it will be better for me to arrange for your investment after seeing Foster & Braithwaite as I can do it just as well by letter. You ought to have kept those bonds.

I called on Mrs. Pat [Campbell] this afternoon. I am to call again Thursday and try to settle about the play.

Yours affectionately.

Том.

[P.S. :] Lady Jeune is much interested in your bicycling.[1]

## LETTER NO. 30

Savile Club, 107, Piccadilly. W.
Wednesday morning [February 5, 1896].

My dear Em :

Post-card received. I am going back to Max Gate this afternoon : and intend to run up again from next Saturday to Monday, to meet a manager.[2] As there is no reason for me to stay on through the week I thought this the best plan. I went to Mrs. [Montagu] Crackanthorpe's masked ball with Lady Jeune and Madeleine last night.[3] It was the most amusing experience I have lately had. I did not recognize people I knew very much : and a lady took *me* down to supper ([it] being leap year) whom to this moment I have not been clear about. They were sorry you could not come. Lady Jeune says it *may* be shingles that you have had, as that goes in a circle round the body. The Miss Thornhills return to Brighton in two or three weeks. Don't have a cheap lodging, as I will willingly

---

[1] In September 1897 Emma was laid up as a result of a bicycle accident.

[2] The possibility of a production of *Tess* was still under discussion.

[3] *Later Years* says (p. 46) that 'he and his wife' attended. This letter shows that Mrs. Hardy did *not* accompany him, and that she was in Brighton and not in London.

pay the difference between the prices. Next Monday I could of course run down [to Brighton] if you wish to see me about anything.

Yours

T.

[P.S. :] Lady Jeune says you can stay there any time by letting her know — except when the room is occupied by a previous comer.[1]

## LETTER NO. 31

Savile Club, 107, Piccadilly. W.
Tuesday [March 2, 1897] 5 p.m.

My dear Em :

I called just now again at the Alexandra [Club], and the Hall porter told me you had got away all right by the 12 something train. This was a relief, for I have been very anxious and unsettled since I got your telegram yesterday morning. I went to the theatre with Lady Jeune, Madeleine and Mr Jones last night, in all the rain : I would much rather have stayed at home, as I was tired : but I did not wish to be disagreeable, and it was kind of them to offer me the fourth place they had. Lady Jeune told me you came to the party, which of course I did not know.

This morning I could not stop a minute when I called, as I was on my way to the St. James's Theatre for the

[1] This is the last letter with an 1896 date, but the absence of further letters should not be misinterpreted. Hardy became ill (a chill followed by rheumatism), and for a week or so he and Mrs. Hardy recuperated at Brighton. In June and July they occupied a rented house in South Kensington, and then took a vacation-tour together in southern England : the Malvern Hills, Worcester, Warwick, Kenilworth, Stratford-on-Avon, and Dover. In mid-September they took an extended tour in Belgium.

copyright performance.[1]  Mr. and Mrs. McIlvaine and a
friend were 'the audience' and duly paid two guineas
each for their seats.  It is a farce which will cost me more
than twenty pounds.

I shall *try* to get home to-morrow by the train reaching
Dorchester by 8.30, but I am not sure.  I feel a dyspeptic
headache gradually brewing, and I should like to be home
when it comes.  If I don't arrive by a little past 9, I shall
not be coming unless I telegraph.  Keep letters.

Yours affectionately,

*    *    *

T.

[There is now a gap of more than two years in the correspondence.  In June 1897, at the time of Queen Victoria's
Diamond Jubilee, Hardy took his wife on a trip to Switzerland.
On their return, they enjoyed bicycling together to various
places in southern England.  And then occurred an event —
with its consequences — about which *The Later Years of
Thomas Hardy* says nothing.  Mrs. Hardy had three brothers.
When the youngest died (in or about 1898), she and Hardy
took into their home at Max Gate this brother's son and
daughter, and for some years Gordon and Lilian Gifford lived
there.  Hardy eventually succeeded in finding London employment for Gordon (see Letter 33).  Lilian is mentioned
in Letter 34, Letter 35, Letter 44, and others.  After the death
of the first Mrs. Hardy, Hardy provided an annuity for Lilian
Gifford, adding substantially to the £220 Mrs. Hardy had
inherited, in order to make up this annuity.  Life at Max
Gate, therefore, took on new aspects in 1898 and 1899 ; but
Hardy was not always there, as the next letter, No. 32, shows.]

---

[1] This was a dramatization of *Tess of the D'Urbervilles*, not Hardy's
own adaptation, but one by Lorimer Stoddard, an American who had
prepared the script in which Mrs. M. M. Fiske starred as Tess in New
York in 1897.  This London performance was no more than a 'reading'
of the text, in order to protect Hardy's copyright in his work.

## LETTER NO. 32

Savile Club, 107, Piccadilly. W.
Saturday [May] 13th [1899].

Dear E : [1]

Would you write to the sender of the Enclosed to say that in my absence from home [2] you write to say that the pencil drawing has (or has not) arrived (as the case may be).

I am sorry to hear of the sprain — bicycling, I suppose. I hope to get back some time next week — it is cold here, and often wet. I have slight toothache, and we have gone back to large fires [at the Club].

I am intending to call this evening at Maida Vale.

T. H.[1]

## LETTER NO. 33

Savile Club, 107, Piccadilly. W.
Monday : noon [? March 12, 1900 ?].

Dear Em :

I have just called here, and received your post card and letters. This morning I called on the Blomfields,[3] and saw Arthur (one of the brothers) and he has just walked with me as far as Grosvenor Square where he had an engagement. It was such a pleasure to hear him give a good account of Gordon. He says he sticks to a piece of work till he has tackled it — and he has put Gordon in the best place in the office — with the two head assistants, where he gains most knowledge. He added : 'We must

[1] Following the 26-month hiatus in the letter-writing, this new salutation, and new signature, appear to mark the passage of time.

[2] *Later Years* says (page 81) : 'they . . . as usual. . . .' This letter shows a different state of affairs. It is apparently the only letter written (or preserved ?) in the year 1899.

[3] Sir Arthur Blomfield, who had been Hardy's employer in 1862, had died toward the end of 1899. His son Arthur had been instrumental in Hardy's finding a position for Mrs. Hardy's nephew, Gordon Gifford.

make an architect of him somehow' — which is encouraging. I think Gordon had better not come to Max [Gate] till later, when the weather [here in London] is trying, as he is in full swing now.

It is bitterly cold here. I called on Mrs. Duff yesterday, at her request, to sign some books for a bazaar. She inquired for you more than once. I have toothache, and think of coming back at the end of week unless inconvenient. Can't you bathe your ancle with something strengthening ? Do not try it by walking, on any account.

T. H.

[P.S. :] There is hardly any London season : no balls, no money : people in mourning. Lady Blomfield is not living in London now : has given up [her] house.

LETTER NO. 34

Savile Club, 107, Piccadilly. W.<br>Thursday [? March 15, 1900 ?].

Dear Em :

I think of returning to-morrow by the train arriving about 6.15 — as I have toothache, headache, etc. I am coming up again the middle of next week for a day or two if possible — or longer. That, I think, will finish London for me this season. I don't see why you cannot stay at the Alexandra Club this year, it being a particularly dull one, and London not full — though I strongly advise you not to come till the cold weather leaves us. Lilian has earache, etc.: everybody has aches in fact. I meant to take her to the Academy, but as she is not well it will be better for you to take her when you come. Gordon is, if he can, coming to lunch here with me to-day, and going on with me to the South Kensington Art Library : I thought I had better show him how to get

out books, etc. — so as to start him there. He is looking
thin in the face, but says he is well. I want also to go
through the Architecture in the Academy with him, but
am not sure if I shall be up to it. A crowd of Americans
and Colonials are coming to London, on their way to
[the] Paris Exhibition but they will be disappointed at its
dulness.

T. H.

[P.S. :] If I cannot come to-morrow I will telegraph.

Keep an eye on the parcel's box, as I am sending home
things.


## LETTER NO. 35

Max Gate, Dorchester [1]<br>Tuesday, December 11 [1900].

Dear Em :

Your Sunday letter came only this morning, and I feel
rather anxious lest you should have broken down under
your [nursing] exertions.[2] There is now no need for
continued effort, as, in settling up bills of a deceased person,
valuation of Probate, etc., the law allows a reasonable
time for relatives to act in. So 'take it stiddy' as they say
here — the case now being no longer one in which a sick
person is dependent on what you do.

Since I am not sure that you may not be gone to London
or elsewhere when this letter arrives, I will not say much.
We are so sorry to hear of the illnesses — and hope you

---

[1] This is apparently the first time that Hardy wrote to his wife *from*
Max Gate, she being the one, this time, to be absent.

[2] Mrs. Hardy had spent October in attendance upon her sister Helen
Catherine (Mrs. Caddell Holder), who died in December 1900 and was
buried on the tenth. After Mrs. Hardy's October absence she had returned
to Max Gate on November 9, but had departed for Cornwall after (or just
before) her sister's death.

are both all right by this time. We pulled down the blinds yesterday from 10 to 12. It was a beautiful day here.

The arrival of the Power of Attorney was a 'little irony' certainly. Yet it is as well that you should have it, before her death, if anybody should make a dispute about it.

I told Lilian about the Cape. But we have decided that, since she cannot go out, the weather being so bad every day, she had better wait till you come back before doing more than she has done — had a 'costume' made at Garge's, as you directed in a previous letter. Packages, when they come, shall be put in East room as you wish.

I had a few lines ['Song of the Soldiers' Wives'] in the *Morning Post* some days ago [November 30, 1900], on the return of the soldiers. I *may* have something in the Christmas Number of the *Sphere*, but am not sure.[1] A short story of mine ['Enter a Dragoon'] is in *Harper's* [*Magazine*] for December [1900].

Yours affectionately,

T.

[P.S. :] One of Mr. Moule's brothers has died — Reverend Frederick.[2] You remember his wife coming to our garden party [last summer]? Lilian and Miss Moule met at Garge's, where they each wanted the same [mourning] things, for the same degree of relationship.

*　*　*

[Eighteen days after Hardy had penned this letter, a poem of his, entitled 'By the Century's Deathbed', appeared in the London *Graphic*, December 29, 1900 (page 956). This is the poem

---

[1] Hardy's poem 'The Lost Pyx' appeared in *The Sphere*, December 22, 1900.

[2] For Frederick Moule, see Letter 63, page 80, footnote 1.

which was later re-entitled 'The Darkling Thrush', in which
he described his mood at this time thus :

> The ancient pulse of germ and birth
> Was shrunken hard and dry,
> And every spirit upon earth
> Seemed fervourless as I.

The cause of this fervourlessness may be conjectured by looking
into the notes written at this time by Rebekah Owen. (She
and her sister Catherine were the 'good judges across the
Atlantic' to whom Hardy had acknowledged his indebted-
ness for the restoration of the caged goldfinch to the pages of
*The Mayor of Casterbridge* : see his preface dated February 1895.)
Mr. Hardy, wrote Rebekah, 'seemed very glad to see me. . . .
I shall . . . try cycling. Mr. Hardy wants me to. Mrs.
Hardy is away. . . . Mr. Hardy, Miss [Lilian] Gifford and I
biked by way of Came Park and Herringstone . . . to the
Weymouth Road, to the top of the Ridgeway Hill. . . .
Then we spun back down it like anything. . . . To Max
Gate to tea, and again Mr. Hardy walked home with me. . . .
[Later :] Mr. Hardy wrote in my books and carried one of
them home for me. We looked over *Wessex Poems* together.'
[When Miss Owen expressed a desire to see Mill Street —
the 'Mixen Lane' of *The Mayor of Casterbridge* — but to see it
after dark, when she couldn't go alone, Hardy offered to
escort her through this slum region, and did. Her notes
continue : 'No action of Emma Lavinia's ever surprises me
and probably does not her husband : but niece [Lilian] says
"Auntie took us by surprise and returned last night." . . .
Mrs. Sheridan says "She leads him a Hell of a life", so I expect
he caught it if she arrived while he was traipsing through the
slums with me. . . . Mrs. Sheridan thinks her half-cracked,
and Mrs. Moule says she is the devil. Mr. Moule's emphatic
"Poor woman, she is phenomenally plain !" and his outbursts
against her general unbearableness amuse us all.'

[Such was the fervourless atmosphere at Max Gate when the Nineteenth Century reached its 'deathbed'. Four months later, Hardy was again back in London.]

LETTER NO. 36

Savile Club, 107, Piccadilly. W.
Friday [April 19, 1901].

My dear Em :

I have just had the *Dorset County Chronicle*. As there was nothing marked I imagine you sent it on account of the carriers.

As I told you, I am at Shirley's [Hotel] — a little top room, looking right away to the city : it is a humble lodging, but does well enough for me by myself : and the place is more reposeful than the larger hotels. I had to sleep in a dismal basement the first night — and have only got this room by catching it quickly in the morning. During the months of April and May, that neighbourhood is crowded with Methodist and other parsons up for the May meetings : and it is necessary to write a fortnight beforehand if you come early in the week. The day to come is any *Saturday*, when many clear out to get home Sunday. As soon as you can let me know when you are coming I will engage a place at the Kingsley or West Central : but try to make it a Saturday : and *do not start* till I reply saying there is accommodation.

I inquired at one or two places for lodgings: they are good enough about Bloomsbury, if the answering the door is not important : but the girls usually do that with a smutty face etc. even where they charge 3/3/- a week for drawing and bedrooms. However I have not inquired far.

Last night I strolled in to [see Sir Henry Irving's presentation of] *Coriolanus*, not knowing what to do

46

with myself. I was impressed by the beauty of the play, and did not regret going, though the [Lyceum] theatre was not quite full — it being a dull play to the ordinary goer.[1]

It is windy and dusty here, and trying to the eyes. I shall be wanting a summer waistcoat which I accidentally left behind in the wardrobe — black and white check — not the green-buff one. When you come will be soon enough : unless I write to have it sent, the weather being now colder again here. I have seen nobody as yet.

Yours affectionately,<br>T.

## LETTER NO. 37

Savile Club, 107, Piccadilly. W.<br>Wednesday [April 24, 1901].

My dear Em :

I have just time to write a line only, as I did not call here [at the Club] till late this afternoon. I am glad you are coming up : it is almost indispensable if we see anybody at all from London when home. You mean by 'going to the Alexandra' that you will sleep there, I conclude. If you can stay on [there] indefinitely we can look for lodgings without your coming to the West Central Hotel : but if you are to be at the Club only for a day or two I had better bespeak a room for you at the hotel, where they are *very* obliging, and anxious to do all they can to accommodate us. But it wears one out rather, living in public. Don't forget your Academy ticket — I will meet you wherever you appoint — if you go straight to the Club perhaps you would prefer me to meet you *in* the Academy : or shall I call at the Club ? I will await instructions : I could probably *now* get a room at the hotel for Saturday — but as you will not want it I

[1] It had opened on April 15 (Monday), and ran until July 20, 1901.

will not inquire. Mine is a front one — *very* noisy all night.

I have seen Charles Blomfield, and will tell you about the [? Gordon] matter when you come.

Yours affectionately,

T.

[P.S. :] You must come by an early train, if you are to get here and see the Academy [exhibition] the same day : there is a quick one I think at 8.20 — but make sure by inquiring — if you come by [the] 10.25 you could not get to the Academy till nearly 4.

LETTER NO. 38

Savile Club, 107, Piccadilly, W.
Saturday [? April 27, 1901].

My dear Em :

I was disappointed that you could not come to-day — the ticket is, unfortunately, too late [now] to be used. I went to the Private View this morning, and may look in again : several people spoke to me — among them Frederic Harrison — who says Mrs. Harrison is at home Tuesdays or Sundays, and would like us to call. I also met Alfred East, A.R.A. He says that if you are interested in [doing] oils he will be pleased to give you any hints, and asks us to his studio.[1] He has some good landscapes

---

[1] Mrs. Hardy had painted water-colour sketches at St. Juliot and had sold them, 'collecting small sums from time to time . . . in order that the historic old church might be rebuilt'. Ten years before the date of this letter, she had done some sketching in Scotland, at which time Hardy had annoyed her by offering to improve the perspective in her sketches. (She retaliated with criticism of his novels, and Sir George Douglas noticed that 'Hardy invariably referred to his wife's criticism with a deference which it did not deserve'.) On September 9, 1892, Mrs. Hardy had gone with Rebekah Owen to sketch Waterston House — the 'fine old Jacobean house' which Hardy had made use of as a residence for his heroine Bathsheba in *Far from the Madding Crowd*.

in the R. A. exhibition this year. I also met the Abbeys who are at home Sundays.[1] Gosse says that his daughter Sylvia is going to be a painter : he was taking her round this morning. Mrs. Henniker has taken a house at Clewes near Windsor and wants us to go down one day. The Lucys have asked me to lunch Tuesday : I did not know you were coming up that day when I accepted, but I will go on from there to the Alexandra. You could have got rooms at the hotel to-day easily. The middle of the week is the difficulty. I too think we had better find lodgings out somewhere by the Royal Oak Bayswater : Bloomsbury is too rackety, and I do not like hotel life much.

The safe headgear is black hat and black feather [2] — all the best people are in black and white : some women, but not ladies exactly, are in bright colours.

I understand now that you *are* going to the Alexandra Club Tuesday, and do *not* want a room at hotel.

Sarah Grand's address is The Grey House, Langton, Tunbridge Wells (it is in *Who's Who*).

Ever affectionately,

T.

## LETTER NO. 39

Savile Club, 107, Piccadilly. W.
25.1.02 [i.e., Saturday, January 25, 1902].

My dear Em :

I have just come in here from the [Londonderry] wedding : an awful crush, many of the invited guests did not get into the church at all, the crowd outside was dense.[3] I saw the Gosses in the press of people in the

[1] Regarding Abbey, see Letter 14, footnote 1, page 20.

[2] Queen Victoria had died on January 22, 1901.

[3] The wedding took place at St. Peter's Church, Eaton Square, London. Lord Stavordale was married to the Countess of Ilchester, only daughter of the Marquis and Marchioness of Londonderry.

drawingroom at Londonderry House afterwards. I told them that you could have been there, but did not care to come to town. I could not get near Lady Londonderry, but I spoke to Lord L. who was, as usual, very nice. I went with Madeleine [Jeune] (bridesmaid) and we should not have got into the church, if Lady Jeune who was also in the carriage had not told the policeman that we had a bridesmaid and *must* get in : so he made the other carriages stand back. Sir Lewis Morris was invited, but could not get in. The Londonderrys are so nice that you may go there any time if you care to. I have given way to Madeleine's wish to go to the theatre to-night — though I would much rather sit here. If any important letter comes Sunday you can send it on to 79 Harley Street. Lady Jeune wants me to stay till Tuesday. She and Sir Francis have gone out of town till Monday, so that only Madeleine and [young] Francis are in the house with me.

Ever yours,

*   *   *

T. H.

[There now occurs a gap of seventeen months in this correspondence. During this interval, Hardy got to work on the first part of *The Dynasts*.]

LETTER NO. 40

The Athenaeum, Pall Mall S.W.
Thursday [June 25, 1903]

Dear Em :

I find that I have left the drawers unlocked in the study, and though they contain nothing of value it will be best to fasten them up. Will you first lock the *two outer front* drawers of the big table with the largest of the two keys hanging in the lock of the small table, cut the keys apart, and lock the large one into one of the small drawers, sending me on the key of the latter.

The middle front drawer of the big table, and the back drawers of the same now unfastened, I do not wish locked — and indeed they cannot be.

The weather is suddenly warm here. I arrived as intended and had tea [with the Duchess of Abercorn] at 13 [Abercorn Place].

Yours<br>T.

## LETTER NO. 41

The Athenaeum, Pall Mall S.W.<br>Saturday [June 27, 1903]

Dear Em :

I was hoping you had got home safely. The weather here has been, if possible, worse : yesterday being a piercingly cold down-pour from morning till night. I could not get home from this club to change my clothes to go to the Royal Society Conversazione — so I did not get there after all. I wanted to see the new developments, but the discomfort was too great. To-day it is very cold still, and I wear my thickest greatcoat, but it does not rain.

I have known about thirty London Junes, but never remember such a one as this.

Lady Jeune and Madeleine each send a note asking me to call if in Town. I have not done so yet, but may look in to-morrow afternoon. There is an invitation to a garden party in Essex ( ! ) sent here for us both : I am replying that we cannot come.

I am thinking of returning the end of next week — feeling rheumatism between the shoulders. They have spotted me at the lodgings, and this makes it rather awkward. I think we might come up together for a week in July perhaps.

Mrs. Moulton has arrived and asks us to come to her

'afternoons'.[1]   Also John Lane (the publisher) invites us both (for his wife) to their tea next Thursday.   I have told them that you have left ;  and that I will try to come, by boat, but I have made no definite engagement.

Yours,<br>T.

### LETTER NO. 42

The Athenaeum, Pall Mall. S.W.<br>Sunday [June 28, 1903].

My dear Em :

On thinking the matter over again I feel that I should like to avoid the racket of going home and coming up to London again this season :  so that I am planning to stay on till you come (if you do).   The only difficulty is (unless you really want me for anything at home) about that lost illustration, the original of which must be in the printer's hands before July 10.   I will therefore try to explain to you how to find it.

The second of the two keys that you separated when you sent me the smaller one the other day, fits the left hand front drawer of the large table.   In that drawer you will find a bunch of miscellaneous keys.   One of these opens the cupboard under the smaller of the two book-cases that *face* the window.   I *think* the drawings for *Wessex Poems* are in a flat packet of brown paper in that cupboard — one of these, 'Leipzig', is the one wanted. They are all stitched together I think, and you must cut the string and separate that one.   If you cannot identify it please refer to *Wessex Poems* in the glazed bookcase, and

---

[1] Louise Chandler Moulton (1854–1909), American novelist and poet, had met Hardy in London in the summer of 1889.   She wrote reviews and literary letters for the New York *Tribune*.   On August 4, 1892, Hardy wrote her :  'Why don't you live in London altogether ?'   Hardy's letters to her are now in the Library of Congress, in Washington ;  the text of these letters has been published in *Hardy in America*, by Carl J. Weber (Waterville :  Colby College Press, 1946).

see the illustration to the 'Leipzig' poem, which will enable you to do so.

In the middle cupboard of the *glazed* bookcase you will find plenty of stiff cardboard to pack it in. Send by parcel post to me at this address. Please pack it safely, as, should that also be lost, there will be no means of replacing the lost illustration.

If you cannot find it in the cupboard I mentioned search in the cupboard with its back to your stairs. (Another key of the bunch unlocks that.) If it is not there look in the bottom drawer of the oak chest of drawers. If not there, try the *back* drawers of the large table that are unfastened. (The fastened one I have the key of, and only cheque books, etc., are there.)

If not found yet, unlock the cupboard under the bookcase on right hand of fireplace. If not yet [found] I must leave you to exercise your own conjectures, for I cannot think further.

It will save me a journey if you do find it.

Ever yours,

T.

## LETTER NO. 43

The Athenaeum, Pall Mall. S.W.

Thursday, July 2 [1903].

My dear Em :

*Do not send on any more letters* — as I must return [home] Saturday. Americans have invaded my lodgings, and I cannot move elsewhere in this hot weather. There are other reasons too why I have had enough of Town for the present.

It does not matter that Bessie [the cook at Max Gate] is away, as one does not want much in this heat. I ate no dinner yesterday, and although I had to undergo the fatigue of taking Lilian to the Academy crush, I felt no worse. It was such a novelty and a delight to her that I was so glad

I took the trouble : she never saw anything at all like it before, poor child, and though I felt past it all, I enjoyed it in an indirect way through her eyes.

I went to the wedding of A H H. yesterday, and just shook hands with him as he came out of Church, but I did not go to the reception. We were both invited — just at the last moment, as he did not know either of us was in town.

I do absolutely nothing now.

Ever affectionately,

T.

[P.S. : Mrs.] Dorothy A[llhusen, daughter of Lady Jeune] asks me to go to the theatre with her next week : but I have, of course, declined.

I have had no letters from Bockhampton for weeks — so did not know of Mrs. F.'s death till you told me.

## LETTER NO. 44

Max Gate.
Friday morning, 13 November [1903].

Dear Em :

I have received your two cards [from Dover] and Bessie wrote [you] yesterday, posting her letter before 5.30, in the hope that you would get it this morning. Enclosed was a letter which had come. Other things by post have been only circulars, and the butcher's bill. A large envelope came from Longmans (bookseller) which does not seem of a kind to send on — but I will if you wish.

Bessie will have told you of [the cat] Markie's experiences. She is not back [from the vet's] yet, but will be Saturday I believe. Snowdove [another cat] strolls about, and is very friendly. Abbot [1] disappeared about

[1] I have been unable to identify him ; he is mentioned again in the letters of November 21 and 26, 1903.

the same time that you did and it has been very lonely here — suitable for finishing my proofs — which are getting towards the end.[1] I could go to London or anywhere in a week or so, I think.

I bicycled to the top of Ridgway Hill yesterday afternoon for some air. The roads are still very good here. I suppose you have examined the works of the new Admiralty harbour which is to make a great naval station of Dover ; and I can imagine the light of Cape Grisnez winking as usual. I am going to get this posted at once (12 o'clock) as it is a day and half's post to Dover from here.

Yours<br>T.

[P.S. :] The postcard view you send is a beautiful one. Kind love to Lilian : hope to see her soon.

## LETTER NO. 45

Max Gate<br>Monday [November 16, 1903], 12 o'clock

Dear E :

Bessie wrote [you] last night enclosing a note — nothing else here worth sending on. I received your card of Saturday, with the enclosures, this morning — there having been no afternoon post yesterday.

I am paying baker, washing, and milkman as directed. Poor Marky is not even home yet — but will come probably at the end of the week. Bessie says she is happy enough [at the vet's], in a large cage with straw etc. It seems that there was danger of gangrene if her foot had not been dressed every day. The others [i.e., the other cats] are well, and friendly with each other, but they are all learning to get inside the [fireplace] fender on the warm bricks.

---

[1] Part I of *The Dynasts*.

The great event of this morning has been the shifting of a large apple-tree from the old fruit garden to the new orchard. It took two men to lift [it], but I think it will grow : the other trees were preventing it bearing in its original place.

I went to the [Town] Hall on Saturday, a local case which has caused some excitement having come before us. Mr. Duke's ricks at Woodsford were all burnt one night — eight or ten large corn stacks — the whole produce of his farm this year having been destroyed — value £1000 — enough corn wasted to have fed 100 families through the winter. There is no proof that the man did it who has been apprehended, though he probably did. We committed him to the Assizes where I fancy he may get off.

I don't think we can go to the Zangwill wedding. When you come back will be soon enough to reply, if you come this week : if not I will write. You have probably replied to Mrs. Rowland Hill — so I will not.

I do not know if Paris may not give you colds this time of the year. You remember we were once there in November, and what a cold I had — but you must use your own judgment. I shall have finished the proofs this week — and should like to go away for a few days, but do not put yourself out on that account, as I may not care to go after all. Mother is much better, and will probably come downstairs for a little while to-day.[1]

That ballad of mine — 'A Trampwoman's Tragedy' — is out in this month's *North American Review*. Gosse writes enthusiastically about it. I shall get this posted before 2 o'clock, in the hope that you may get it by the morning. I am glad to hear that Lilian likes being there — shall be glad to see her again whenever fate ordains.

Yours

T.

---

[1] Hardy's mother, Jemima Hand Hardy, died on April 3, 1904.

[P.S. :] Pretor's pictures, china, etc. are come — he says he is quite brilliant now in his surroundings, and calls his lodgings the New Jerusalem.

## LETTER NO. 46

Max Gate, Dorchester
[Thursday] November 19 [1903].

Dear Em :

I have just received your card from Calais, and reply at once. Nothing has happened here since I wrote to you at Dover two or three days ago. But the weather has turned frosty, and this morning it is very cold — Calais is I should think a cold place. I have not yet had my last pages of proof so cannot leave home. I told you in my letter what I thought about the Zangwill wedding — i.e. that I could not go. Markie has not come back yet. Bessie went to see her yesterday. We expect to have her Saturday. If you did not get the letter I wrote Monday, and posted in the afternoon, you had better call for it at the lodgings when you return to Dover.

Love to Lilian.

Yours
T.

## LETTER NO. 47

Max Gate.
Saturday [November 21, 1903] 11 a.m.

Dear Em :

I received your card last night, by calling at the P.O., otherwise it would have been delivered here this morning. The event of the morning is that Charles has fetched Markie, who is now wandering about the house gradually recalling the place. She wants to be friendly with Snow-dove, and remembers him perfectly, but he does not remember her — at least spits at her — as also does Pixie :

but Comfy is indifferent. I may want to go to London for one night next week, but I do not like to be away longer. I finished the proofs [of *The Dynasts, Part I*] last night. In returning [from France] you will have to be ruled by weather : it is now practically winter, with all its treacheries. Our two or three hard frosts have passed, and it is getting windy, but is not cold.

You must be mistaken in thinking we stayed at the hotel you are in — as we have never put up in Calais to my recollection, though we have passed through. I fancy you are thinking of the Hôtel Christol, at Boulogne, where we did stay once. I wonder if you have looked for the celebrated Hôtel Dessein of Sterne's *Sentimental Journey* ? The guide book says that the present Hôtel Dessein is not the old one, which is now turned into Baths, Museum, etc. Calais, as you know, belonged to us for 200 years down to [Queen] Mary's reign. It has always had the reputation of a place where the English are fleeced, but that was before railways. — I see in Shelley's Life [1] that when he and Mary landed [at Calais in 1814] after crossing in the boat on the day of their flight, they 'walked over the sands to the inn,' but the name of the inn is not given : it was there that Mrs. Godwin overtook them, and vainly requested Mary to return with her. The inn seems, anyhow, to have been near the sands.[2]

Abbot writes this morning from London. He goes to St. Paul's every day. He says nothing about returning yet. I am going to post this before 2, in the hope that you may get it to-morrow morning. But for the circumstance of Markie's arrival and demand of attention I should have posted [this] before 11. Mention the *town* when you give your address as I am not sure sometimes [where you are].

[1] Hardy owned J. C. Jeaffreson's *The Real Shelley*, 2 vols., 1885, and Mrs. Julian Marshall's *Life and Letters of Mary Shelley*, 2 vols., 1889.
[2] N. I. White says that it *was* Dessein's Hotel.

Also leave your address when you come away, in case a late letter arrives, but the best plan is to stay to the day you say you are going to leave on. Wherever you go (if you go anywhere else) it will be best to keep near the sea, as you may get a cold inland, particularly at Paris.

I posted a card to you at the 'Poste Restante' — so if you have called you will have received it. The Miss Shirleys have called, and I have just finished reading Mr. Faulkner's new novel — an interesting romance of the old-fashioned sort. Love to Lilian : and a pleasant crossing.

Yours<br>T.

[P.S. :] Remember not to overrun money in hand, as I cannot send cheque to be quickly cashed, as in London. It would take some days to get [money] into your hands.

## LETTER NO. 48

The Athenaeum, Pall Mall. S.W.<br>Tuesday evening [November 24, 1903]. 5.30

Dear Em :

I am up here for a day or two — having just arrived. Am sleeping at the West Central [Hotel]. I shall stay till Thursday or Friday — so far as I know — possibly go back Saturday. Write here (if you do write in time for the days I mention) as the room at the Hotel is a bad one and I may change.

It is much colder here than in Dorset. I received this morning your letter written yesterday — so that you must have posted it in time for the day boat.

In haste<br>T.

[P.S. :] Love to L[ilian].

## LETTER NO. 49

The Athenaeum, Pall Mall. S.W.
Thursday [November 26, 1903].

Dear Em :

Your letter was delivered here this morning, but mine, written from here, should have reached you by the next morning's delivery instead of the afternoon. However it makes no difference, but it shows that the post cannot quite be depended on when it has to cross the water.

I went to St. Paul's service yesterday afternoon with Abbot and Mrs. McCarthy, and afterwards up into the organ loft, where Sir G. Martin, the organist, explained to us the instrument — the enormous size of it, and completeness of control, being very interesting. I went to his house afterwards, and had tea with him and Lady Martin. They are extremely nice people, and knew your uncle when he was Archdeacon there. Their house is in a secluded garden, with old trees etc. — an absolutely peaceful place, though close to the Cathedral.

Mrs. McCarthy was sorry you were not in London. She says the advice you gave her about salt was beneficial. Her address is 8 Cheyne Gardens, Chelsea, if you should like to call [while] passing through [London].

I am calling upon nobody, so have no news to tell. I think of returning [home on] Saturday, though I shall, I hope, call at Abercorn Place before I leave. You were fortunate to see the M.P.s — the papers here were full of their going.[1] In the National Gallery this morning I looked at 'Old Calais Gate', by Hogarth. Is the gate still in existence? Hope Lilian is well, and that you continue as vigorous as the [sea] air has made you. If you *wished*, you could go to Boulogne by train and back in a day — it

[1] On November 26, 1903, the London *Times* carried an article (page 3) reporting the 'British Parliamentary Visit to Paris'.

is about 25 miles off, I think. I shall lunch here, and, I think, go to the Abbey this afternoon.

Yours<br>T.

[P.S. :] Mrs. Ayrton's address (if you should like to write and say you are sorry you could not be at the wedding) is 41 Norfolk Square, Hyde Park.

Posted about 1.


## LETTER NO. 50

Max Gate.<br>Sunday [November 29, 1903].

Dear Em :

I have got back from London — returning last night at 7 — by that excellent train which leaves Waterloo at 4.10 (Southwestern). I don't know if you took a return ticket : if so, it is only available for a month. The two last days in London of incessant rain gave me influenza, of course : and I can do no more to-day than sit and sneeze into the fire. This letter is written at intervals between. I will disinfect it by holding it to the fire before folding it up.

*I think your wise course would be not to stay there much longer :* as winter weather may bring an illness, and from my experience Friday night and yesterday I know the misery of being unwell at a hotel — much more seriously [if] ill, alone, with a foreign doctor. Calais is not by any means a place to winter in. I should, of course, be delighted for Lilian to come on here, but my advice is that you do not stay there alone. Perhaps your plans may be influenced by the news Bessie tells me — that she is not going to be married after all, but will stay on here with us. This will enable us to go away anywhere after Christmas— not to London, but to some place where influenzas do not abound.

I was going to call at 13 Abercorn Place on Friday evening to see them, but the rain was heavy, and this cold coming on, so that I stayed in, and have not seen them at all.

I should not, if I were you, stay in London more than a night or two passing through, otherwise you may get influenza likewise.

I think it highly probable that you are in the very hotel occupied by Shelley and Mary, and where the celebrated interview with the pursuing Mrs. Godwin took place.

At the Athenaeum [Club] I met Henry James, saw Kipling, talked to Humphrey [sic] Ward, was introduced to the Vice-Chancellor of Oxford University (who is a member) etc. I practically lived at the club. I lunched one day with the Macmillans at their business-place, St. Martin's Street.[1] It is a very large establishment, with an immense number of clerks. They have a million books there, and room for two millions.

The four cats are quite well and were glad of my return. Pixie particularly, as she thinks I understand her.

Yours,

T.

[P.S. :] I have sent two papers — I hope you got them.

*   *   *

[Now follows a puzzling period of fifty-two months — nearly four and a half years — during which we have no letters from Hardy to his wife. Why ? It is hard to believe that he wrote none. Mrs. Hardy may have discarded them at the time of

---

[1] Macmillan & Co. were preparing to publish *The Dynasts, Part First*. The book was ready by December 1903, but was held up by the slowness of the printers who were preparing an American edition. As a result of this delay, the book did not appear until January 13, 1904.

their receipt, or she may have lost them during some of her travels, or she may have subsequently destroyed them. We shall probably never know the true explanation.

[It is unfortunate that this gap coincides with an extremely important period in Hardy's life, during which he was bringing *The Dynasts* to completion. It is highly desirable, therefore, that in our attempts to penetrate the darkness we set up as many lighted signposts as we can along the poet's path. We have already taken notice of the fact that in 1904, 1906, and 1908, he gave copies of the three parts of *The Dynasts* to Florence Henniker. We can now add some additional facts. In 1904 Mrs. Henniker came to call at Max Gate and brought with her a twenty-five-year-old friend, Miss Florence Emily Dugdale. This young lady had literary ambitions and eventually became known as the author of half a dozen or more children's books, such as *The Adventures of Mr. Prickleback* and a *Book of Baby Birds*. Miss Dugdale's residence in London made it possible for her to offer to be of service to Hardy, in connection with his further researches for *The Dynasts* ; and, as he went on with the composition of Part II in 1905, he availed himself of her offer. She looked up various details in the British Museum and made it clear that she took delight in thus being of service. She also possessed one other useful skill : she knew how to use the typewriter. (Later on, she was sometimes referred to as Hardy's secretary, but she herself denied ever having been a paid or hired secretary.) She made various subsequent visits to Max Gate, and there noticed what seemed to be Hardy's callous indifference to his wife. At this date, Miss Dugdale had had no way of learning how one topic after another had been crossed off the list of things the Max Gate couple could talk about. Early in their married experience Hardy had learned to keep quiet on the subject of social graces. Like Winterborne in *The Woodlanders* Hardy was 'unrefined' ; she was 'accomplished'. When Mrs. Hardy denounced his uncouth lack of polish, he learned to keep quiet. When she found fault with his unorthodox religious views ('The Cathedral was a very good place four or five centuries ago ; but it is played out now' : in *Jude the Obscure*), Hardy learned to bridle his tongue. When, after tossing *Jude* aside, Mrs. Hardy gave up further interest in his books, he learned to turn elsewhere for literary talk. He could discuss books with Gosse but not with Emma. (Sir George Douglas remembered her saying of *The Trumpet-Major* : 'Yes, that's one of the pretty ones !') One by one, the topics of conversation had been crossed off the list, until what was left was the weather, wedding receptions, and cats. What Miss Dugdale took to be indifference was the better part of wisdom — the result of thirty years' domesticity with Emma Lavinia.

[In April 1907, when the Hardys were in London, he received the offer of two theatre tickets. He replied : 'My wife is out of town . . . so I cannot answer for her. I question however if she will go, as she hardly ever goes out at night.' On June 22, 1907, they went together to attend the Royal Garden Party at Windsor Castle. Thanks to the fact that the French portrait-painter, Jacques-Émile Blanche, and his wife went with the Hardys, we know what happened, for Blanche never forgot the incident. On their arrival at Windsor, it was clear that the large number of persons arriving for the Court festivity was far beyond the capacity of the conveyances waiting at the station to carry the guests up the steep hill to the Castle. Mrs. Hardy, wearing a long green veil, took a place in one of the royal carriages and invited Madame Blanche to come with her.

The latter declined, urging Hardy to take the seat and spare himself in the July-like heat. The author had just passed his sixty-seventh birthday and looked even older. Rheumatism had so lamed his back that on a previous occasion he had found it impossible to walk downstairs. He was obviously frail. Other guests headed for Windsor Castle followed Madame Blanche's example in urging Hardy to ride. But Mrs. Hardy settled the matter. 'Mr. Hardy

ride ? That walk up the hill in the sun will do him a lot of good.'
So up the stony hill Thomas Hardy and the portrait-painter trudged
on foot, following the open carriage with its driver in King Edward's scarlet livery and its lady in a green veil, seated under a
bright silk umbrella. (*Hardy of Wessex*, 1940 ; page 170.)

[In this same June of 1907, Hardy inscribed a copy of
*Wessex Poems* 'To Miss Florence Dugdale, with the Author's
kind regards'. A month later he gave her a copy of *The
Rubáiyát*, inscribed simply : 'F. E. D. from T. H.' Early in
1908, Emma Hardy was confined to bed with bronchitis, and
it may have been about this time that the Hardys discovered
that Florence Dugdale could do lots of things besides typewrite
and consult books in the British Museum. She could run a
house, give instructions to the servants, keep things in order.
Later in 1908 Hardy gave her a copy of Barnes's *Poems* — the
edition which Hardy edited — inscribed to 'Miss F. E. Dugdale,
with the Editor's kind regards'. In 1909 he gave her a copy of
*The Mayor* and still later (to look, for a moment, beyond the
four-year gap we are here dealing with) he gave her a copy of
*Tess* inscribed 'To Florence Emily Dugdale, with best wishes
from Thomas Hardy'.

[As we shall see when we reach the letter which Hardy
wrote to Emma on July 2, 1908, matters had by that date
progressed to a point at which Florence Dugdale was installed
at Max Gate, in charge of the house and servants, while the
Hardys were discussing a midsummer visit to London. Either
Emma did not keep all his letters at this time, or Hardy wrote
to her less frequently. He did write, however, and wrote in
such terms as to make it impossible to apply the word 'estrange-
ment' to their relationship, unless we define that word in
quite a different sense from its meaning when applied, for
example, to Shelley and Harriet, or to Meredith and Mary
Ellen Nicolls, or to other 'estranged' couples.]

## LETTER NO. 51

The Athenaeum, Pall Mall. S.W.
Monday 25 May [1908].

Dear E : [1]

I have just received your card. I am thinking of returning the latter part of this week — I don't quite know which day — either Thursday, Friday, or Saturday.

I have seen some nice lodgings on Richmond Hill, but of course they are ten miles out of London and a quarter-hour's walk to them from Richmond Station. But there are plenty of flys [sic], and it is a pleasant spot. Before I come back I am going to look about Kilburn, St. John's Wood, etc. which would be handier, though lodgings there are grimy compared with Richmond.

I think it would be safer for you to go your Club and stay a few days first — as I shall not be able to get to Town by June 10 — (which is Whit-Wednesday : London full of country visitors) as I go to Lord Curzon's on the 8th and Lady St. Helier wants me to go on to her at Poplar Farm, near Newbury (only twelve miles from Curzon's) after I leave him which would take me on into the next week.[2]

Do not post anything after Wednesday next, unless I write. Also do not post anything more to the Savile : only here, to the Athenaeum.

If anything occurs to alter what I have said above I will let you know.

Yours
T. H.

[P.S. :] Look out for parcels. One big one [is coming] by railway.

[1] From this date on, Mrs. Hardy is reduced (in the salutation) to this mere initial, nor does he ever again sign himself 'affectionately' or use his name. From now on, he too is a mere initial (or initials).

[2] In the final outcome, the Hardys took no house at all this year.

[Second P.S. :] I have a tiny back room at the top, at the West Central Hotel — where they are crowded — as everywhere else this week.

T. H.

## LETTER NO. 52

The Athenaeum, Pall Mall. S.W.<br>Sunday [June 28, 1908].

Dear E :

Have you decided on the day that you would like to come to Town. As I imagine from what you said that Wednesday the 8th or Thursday the 9th would suit you, I have asked at the hotel if we can have a double-bedded room for both of us, or an extra single-bedded room for you, about those dates, and they say yes — it will be possible for the next two or three days, though they are booking fast ahead. The Hotel is just now crowded, and of course the front rooms are terribly noisy — Hyde Park Mansions was quietude by comparison — the windows having to be kept open on account of the heat.

Say what day, and what kind of room you would like, and I will do my best.

I dined at Mrs. [Frederick] Macmillan's and at Mrs. Crackanthorpe's — both small quiet parties — only four at the latter.

There will be two or three dividend warrants coming about July 5, which put by safely somewhere.

Yours,<br>T.

## LETTER NO. 53

The Athenaeum, Pall Mall. S.W.<br>July 2 [1908] : Thursday.

Dear E :

As you will have learnt from my telegram, my not keeping the engagement with Sir H. Herkomer was his secretary's fault. However I have set it all right with him.[1]

We are invited to dine at the Frederick Macmillans on the 14th. It is simply by word of mouth, owing to my not being able to go to their dinner on the 10th. I have accepted, and have told him that as soon as I hear from you I will let him or her know whether you can come or not. So please say. I have told the Messrs. Smith (at the Hotel) that you are coming on Tuesday, and have arranged for a room with two beds. They say they can alter it if that does not suit, and seem anxious to oblige, though the Hotel is crammed.

*I* had the card inviting us to lunch at the Stephen Collins's, and left it somewhere in the study I think. The reply was to be sent to William Watkins, which I duly did. As you are coming to London perhaps you had better not worry about the lunch, and reply to Watkins that you are unable to attend. His address is 62 London Wall, London, E.C.

The wedding you tell me of must be I think that of Colonel Mount-Batten's son by his first wife, though I am not sure. I shall have left London before July 21, I imagine ; and am not inclined to go anyhow.

Florence has money to pay Trevis this coming Saturday, and in the right hand drawer of my large study table you will I think find 7/- in a packet, which give her for him next week. If you cannot find it give her 7/- and I will repay you.

I feel uneasy about forwarding letters after you have left, and think you had better tell Florence to *keep* them, and not forward any. I *could* run down for a day before I go back for good, and then I could look them over.

Did you see in the list of the birthday honours that

---

[1] Sir Hubert Herkomer was about to paint Hardy's portrait. In 1891 he had drawn some of the pictures for the *Graphic*'s serialization of *Tess*.

Greenhill is made a knight.  He must now hunt up an American heiress, who will jump to be 'my lady'.

I went to the Franco British Exhibition for an hour an evening or two ago.  It is like a lot of wedding cakes set out on a grass plot — fearfully wearying as you have to walk miles to go over it.  There are wheeled chairs at half a crown an hour, but not many, and sometimes they are difficult to get.

I suppose the garden is quite dried up.  It was unfortunate that the tank should have been cleared out when it was.

Yours<br>T.

[P.S. :]  I went to the unveiling [by Lord Curzon] of the Mrs. Craigie memorial [at University College] yesterday.

## LETTER NO. 54

The Athenaeum, Pall Mall. S.W.<br>Friday [July 3, 1908].

Dear E :

Card and letters received.  The heat here is very trying, and if this weather continues you will be hardly able to do anything if you do come up.  Should you not feel 'fit', I will get over the difficulty of having engaged the room. The Smiths are very obliging : moreover so many more people come than they can accommodate that it will be let again immediately.  I should not present a bouquet to Mrs. C. if I were you : it ought of course be done by a male member of the Club : upon the whole I don't think I should go, unless you would particularly *like* to.  I sat to Sir Hubert von Herkomer this morning for the first time.

Yours<br>T.

## LETTER NO. 55

The Athenaeum, Pall Mall. S.W.
Monday [July 6, 1908].

Dear E :

Your card has come, and though I should like to see you in London I feel, to tell the truth, rather anxious about your venturing up here. The hotel is so very noisy just now, and the heat so great, that I fear you will be prostrated. Don't you think you ought to wait till the question of [your] being able to *see* is settled — I mean till you know how much good the spectacles are going to do.

We had a terrific thunderstorm early Saturday morning. Of course it woke me, as I am in a small room high up, and obliged to pull up the blind and open the window as wide as I can for air, so the lightning literally flamed into my room. I thought it meant the end of the hot weather, but it is warm again to-day.

I will tell Mrs. Frederick Macmillan that you are not coming. If I had not accepted I could have come home a few days sooner. I am getting to feel that I have had enough of Town, and Herkomer will have finished with me in a few more sittings I suppose.

I go to Cambridge [for the Milton Tercentenary] Friday — sleep there, and probably return [to London on] Saturday.

Will you wire to me to-morrow morning between 9 and 10 to say which you are going to do. On account of the uncertainty I cannot say that you will have a nice room. Address the telegram 'Hardy, West Central Hotel, Southampton Row London.' Keep the Bank of England letters and lock them up with the others.     Yours

T.

P.S. I would rather take you to Cornwall than about London. I shall be out Wednesday etc. at the Studio,

and shall be obliged to leave you to your own resources.
I enclose Philip Gosse's reply for his [wedding] present.

T.

## LETTER NO. 56

The Athenaeum, Pall Mall. S.W.
Monday [July 13, 1908].

Dear E :

Letters received. It has poured with rain all the morning here, but is drier now (afternoon). I have rather got mixed with my engagements to sit to Sir H. H. and the others : but I suppose I shall come home some time next week.

I had a good time for the two days at Cambridge — (I daresay you read what the *Times* said about it).[1] But I was shown over the Colleges etc., on the Saturday and am rather tired still. I saw the Charles Moules,[2] and they asked for you, and for the cats' welfare.

Yours,

T.

## LETTER NO. 57

The Athenaeum, Pall Mall. S.W.
Thursday morning [July 16, 1908] 11 o'clock.

Dear E :

I have just called here, and received your card. I *am* getting tired of London, and think of returning Monday, or perhaps Tuesday — Monday if I can. The difficulty about the portrait is that Sir H. H. has so many engagements that I have only about two sittings a week of about an hour each — so that much time is covered when ten or a dozen are required. However, this is the last week, and

[1] On July 11 the *Times* had printed (p. 11) a report of the Milton Tercentenary celebration (July 10 and 11, 1908), and on the 13th printed a review (p. 9) of the performance of Milton's *Comus* on the 10th. Hardy met Robert Bridges, Poet Laureate, at this time.

[2] For Charles Moule, see Letter 63, footnote 1, page 80.

what remains unfinished he is going to do in the autumn. I am going down to his house at Bushey to-morrow evening, I believe, as he wants to see me by lamp-light — on some question of shadows.

I went to the Gosse wedding Tuesday, as they would have been hurt if neither of us had gone, but I stayed only a few minutes. Henry James sat next me in the church.[1] I have to lunch at the House of Commons to-morrow, which is my last 'function' I think.[2]

Yours,<br>T.

[P.S. :] I can't *think* why the servants' room should require disinfecting, as nobody has ever been ill there.

T.

\*   \*   \*

[Now occurs a two-month gap in the letter-writing. Emma had decided that she would like a new bedroom constructed at Max Gate, and Hardy had dutifully agreed to the 'troublesome job'. While the work was being done, Emma went off to Calais, France, for a month, during which Hardy wrote her seven letters.]

## LETTER NO. 58

Max Gate.<br>15:9:'08 [September 15, 1908]

My dear E :

I received your letter yesterday afternoon (4 o'clock post) and sent on the *Times* last night. I will send another

---

[1] On Tuesday, July 14, 1908, Philip H. G. Gosse, son of Edmund Gosse, and Miss Gertrude Agnes Hay were married in the church of St. Mary Abbots, Kensington.

[2] This letter, with its report of the sittings to Herkomer, a trip to Bushey, the wedding in Kensington, and a lunch at the House of Commons, provides a useful contradiction of the statement in *Later Years* (page 133) that, after the Milton Tercentenary, 'the remainder of the month was spent in Dorset.' Obviously it wasn't.

if it should contain anything important. I enclose all the
letters that have come. I am glad you are comfortable
in Calais. Six francs a day inclusive is, I should think,
as cheap as if you were in lodgings and provided for
yourself.

I have not been anywhere yet, as I do not like to leave
till the window, etc., is in hand, at any rate. They are
making it at the shop, and will come about the end of
this week to begin putting it in. It will be rather a troublesome job, as the slope of the roof has to be moved back, to
enlarge the room over the W.C. It will I think be a good
bedroom when it is done. All we fear is rain while the
slates are off, but [brother] H[enry] is going to put a
tarpaulin over the hole if he can fix it. We have taken
up your carpet and cleared everything away.

It is very dull here, and I am glad of it, as it would be
awkward if people were to come [calling] now. I have
put some boards into the man's room to spread the apples
on, but it rains this morning, and I cannot get in some of
the riper, as I had intended.

Marky is getting quieter, and as the weather is chillier
she and the other two live all together in the kitchen
mostly. The excitement of the morning has been Kitsey's
conduct : she is looking for a bed for her kittens, and has
been up to Jane's room, and torn her Sunday hat in rents,
so that she cannot wear it any more. She says it cost
4s/11d, so I have given her 5/- to buy another, and she is
quite content. Kitsey looks on unconcerned.

I could, of course, run over to Calais if I should have
to be in London for anything, but it does not seem worth
while to go all the way from here. Calais was called in
the time of James the first 'sluttish and monstrous dear' —
and the guide book says that the description still holds
good, in the opinion of some. (This was, however,
written thirty years ago.) I daresay you know that the

principal gate, leading from the seaside into the town, is the one painted by Hogarth.

You must mind not to be too friendly with strangers, as you don't know who's who in a town through which the worst (and no doubt the best) of the earth pass on their way out of our country when it gets too hot for them.

Yours,

T.

[P.S.:] To-day's *Times* says that Bosworth Smith yesterday underwent 'successfully a serious operation in London, and the Doctors are so far thoroughly satisfied with his condition'.

## LETTER NO. 59

Max Gate

Saturday morning [September 19, 1908].

Dear E :

I am sending on all the letters that have come. The rest are circulars. Nothing of any account has happened. A telegram came from Mrs. [A. Brinsley] Sheridan yesterday asking us to lunch [at Frampton Court] : I told her you were away, but that I would come. I am starting in about an hour. I had intended to bicycle, but it is too wet, so I am going by train. The only people whom you did not inform [when you hurried off to Calais] that the party [you had planned to give] was put off were the Basketts, and they came all the way from Evershot : unfortunately I happened to be out, so they had to go back without even a cup of tea. I wrote yesterday to Mrs. Baskett, apologising, and telling her that you were abroad. I hardly think it necessary that you should write also.

They are digging in the [Dorchester] Amphitheatre, but have found very little yet, beyond a few coins, bits of pottery etc. that show the construction to have been

Roman. I cannot hear how Bosworth Smith is getting on. Marky merely sits in the kitchen because she likes the fire : she and Kitsy lie on the hearthrug in the stroke of it.

Yours,<br>T.

## LETTER NO. 60

Max Gate : Thursday.<br>[September 24, 1908].

Dear E :

I have just received your card, also *Daily Mail* (which you need not send as it only contains the news in the other papers). The rain has been so incessant (except Monday) that we cannot take off the [roof] slates yet, and are waiting to see what next week will be like. The woodwork is being got ready as far as possible. Kitsy is having her kittens this afternoon. We are going to drown them to-morrow morning except one. You must remember that the price of the *Times* abroad is more than here — double I think.

There have been no kitchen accidents. Daisy nurses Marky, who seems to like it. The only callers have been Mrs. (Colonel) Barnes and Mrs. Rowland Hill. I was out on both occasions. Mr. Evans the Chemist called upon me this afternoon about the *Trumpet-Major* play, which is to be produced about the middle of November.[1] I

---

[1] On February 4, 1908, a lecture was given at Dorchester by A. M. Broadley on the subject 'Napoleon and the Invasion of England'. As a dramatic and musical supplement to this lecture, a scene from Hardy's *The Trumpet-Major* — the amusing party at Overcombe Mill — was given by members of the Dorchester Debating and Dramatic Society. This sketch proved so successful that it was proposed that the entire novel be dramatized. The adaptation was made by A. H. Evans, who (among manifold other activities) conducted a pharmacy in Dorchester near the King's Arms Hotel. (He was the father of Maurice Evans, the Shakespearean actor, and of Miss Evelyn L. Evans, later [in 1961 — ] the custodian of the Hardy Birthplace at Higher Bockhampton.) Evans's dramatization of *The Trumpet-Major*

bicycled to Weymouth Monday and had tea with Mrs. Frampton and Miss Fetherstonhaugh. They are leaving to-morrow. I think I told you I went to Mrs. Sheridan's : she had an American lady there. Our day at the Amphi-theatre was drenching, with sticky chalk-mud half way up to our knees : I am sending a *Dorset County Chronicle* that you may read the account. Mr. and Mrs. Faulkner, who are staying at Weymouth, were present — drenched and plastered like the rest : she said she wished you had been there. I lunched with them at the King's Arms. The birds do not seem to want crumbs, everything being so moist and food so plentiful. I cannot gather in many apples, as they are seldom dry enough. I think I have told you everything up to now.

Yours,

T.

PS. I enclose the only letter : all the rest [are] circulars.

### LETTER NO. 61

Max Gate. Wednesday evening.

30 September [1908].

Dear E :

Instead of sending on your dividend warrant, which came this morning, I asked the Bank to-day (my bank, the Wilts & Dorset) to send you ten pounds : they said two £5 Bank of England notes would be the easiest way of sending it, and quite safe in an official envelope. So it will arrive with, or before, this letter. If they will not take the notes at the hotel there are English banks in Calais, where

was given in Dorchester, November 18 and 19, 1908, and thus inaugurated what became almost an annual event — the presentation of a dramatic adaptation by A. H. Evans of one of the Wessex novels. The first World War put an end to the Evans series ; but in 1920 the practice was resumed, with adaptations made by T. H. Tilley of Dorchester.

you can change them. But mind to go to a respectable place, where they will not take you in. You can get English sovereigns, or for *each* £5 note six napoleons and about six francs, if you want it in French money. To make up the £17 there will be £7 left, which I think will be enough for housekeeping here, as it is on a very small scale. Let me know if the notes arrive safely.

The heat here to-day, after the rain of Sunday etc. has been tropical : not a cloud : they say it has been the hottest day of the year. I hope it may continue, as we have the roof open now, and the [installation of the] dormer [window is] in full progress. It is troublesome, but worth doing. I am glad you are not here in the mess and hammering, though no dirt or dust comes down into the house.

We had a fright on Monday night about Marky. She slipped out of the dining room about 7 o'clock, and absolutely disappeared. The servants and I wandered about the garden with lanterns till nearly 12.: I came down at 1, and at 4, but could not find her. When they got up at 7 she calmly walked down out of the stable loft. The reason of her affront was that Kitsy thought she wanted to get away her kitten, and flew at her. The kitten (the last one) is now drowned — such a pretty one — white, with black streaks on its back. Marky is now quite happy, and lives mostly in the dining room.

I have given all your messages to Jane : she quite understands, and has gone this afternoon to pay some of the bills. Daisy nurses Kitsy now as a part of her work, till she gets over the loss of her kittens. Mrs. Kinden's son at the cottage was buried to-day — [he was only] sixteen. They sent over to tell you when he died, as they said you had inquired how he was. Mrs. Huxtable called to see you : I do not remember anybody else, but I am keeping the cards. Oh, yes — the Faulkners came yesterday : they are staying at Weymouth, leaving on

Sunday. You need not hurry, as order reigns. Miss May Sinclair says she is coming to see me, but she has not been yet.

Yours,

T.


## LETTER NO. 62

[Max Gate,] Monday morning
[October 5, 1908].

Dear E :

I have received your card. Marky is quite well and satisfied now, and sleeps either on the sofa, or by day, on the dinner waggon, so that you need not be anxious about her. We are in a great mess just now — I mean in the attic where the new window is, not anywhere else — so that it would be awkward for you to come [home] this week. Perhaps you could come over to Dover and stay if you wish to leave Calais. You will have to use the West room for a time until the plaster is dry. Fortunately up to now we have not had a drop of rain while the roof has been open.

Comfy is very comfortably sleeping, but feeble. He went down the lower lawn one sunny day, but could not walk back, and had to be carried. I think it is rheumatism — nothing more.

People have been talking about the heat here during last week : nothing like it for seventy-five years.

Yours

T.


## LETTER NO. 63

Max Gate : [Friday] October 9. 1908.

Dear E :

I have just received your card. I had stopped sending on anything as I was not quite sure if you would be leaving

[Calais], and there was nothing of a pressing kind to send. This evening I have posted three Protestant papers (apparently) and will post others if they come.

There is no news of any importance since I last wrote, except such as you see in the papers. I am sending the *Dorset Chronicle*, which has a notice of your pictures. In to-day's *Times* I have an article on Maumbury Ring, but I do not send it as you have probably seen it by this time.[1]

The cats are very well, Comfy being better again now. Kitsy caught a leveret in the garden on Monday : and we have cooked and eaten it : she seemed quite willing to let us have it. Marky sits on the corner of the dining room table as usual. They do not mind the workmen being here.

I do not see how you can have an afternoon reception this autumn. The porch is pulled down, so we use the side door, the front door being fastened. I felt that if the porch were to be enlarged at all, it must be now : and of course, the days being wet and short, the work will be rather tedious. Owing to the damp weather — for though it was hot last week, nothing seemed to dry — the plaster does not dry in your upstairs room, though the first coat is on, but the glass of the window is not yet in, in order to have a draught to dry the walls. I think you will like the room now, and you can retain it until a room is made for you over the man's room, which will be a matter of time.

As people now know that you are away nobody calls, which is fortunate. I had promised those ladies Miss May Sinclair and her American friend Miss Moss [2] that I would bicycle to Weymouth with them to-day, as I thought I should like a little outing after the drudgery of the

---

[1] In August 1942 this article was republished in book form by the Colby College Library. There are copies of the book in the British Museum, the Bodleian, the Hardy Room in the Dorset County Museum, and in the library of Leeds University.

[2] Mary Moss was the author of an article, 'The Novels of Thomas Hardy', in the *Atlantic Monthly* (98 : 354–367), Boston, September 1906.

hammering here, etc. But it has rained the whole day, so we did not go. They are staying at Wareham.

The Leslies [1] have come back, and I went down to tea yesterday to meet his relative Lady Constance Leslie, an old lady, who was a Damer, you may remember. I had not seen her since I met her at Lady Jeune's many years ago. She told me the story of her sister refusing Louis Napoleon. Mrs. Leslie says she has heard from Becky Owen, who has become a Roman Catholic, much to her sister's distress.[2]

It is very dismal here, and if you come back I do not think you will stay long. However, it will be a great relief to get these jobs done, as they have been upon my mind so long. The servants are very quiet, and attentive about the cats. A woman in Dorchester has murdered her baby.

Yours<br>T.

[P.S. :] Scarlet fever is about here. Bosworth Smith recovers very slowly : it is still doubtful with him. Arthur Symons (the writer, not the Dorchester one) is ill in Italy.

[1] The Rev. Edward C. Leslie was the rector of Came Church, near Dorchester. Mrs. Leslie was the daughter of Hardy's one-time neighbour, Henry J. Moule (1825–1904), who for many years was the curator of the Dorset County Museum. Frederick Moule (mentioned in Letter 35) was a younger brother of Curator Henry Moule ; and Charles Moule (another brother, mentioned in Letter 56) was Senior Fellow and, later, President of Corpus Christi College, Cambridge. He had served Hardy as a model for Angel Clare in *Tess of the D'Urbervilles*. These three brothers were sons of the Rev. Henry Moule (1801–1880) who was Vicar of Fordington in Hardy's youth. Hardy had often attended Mr. Moule's church. When the vicar's grand-daughter Margaret Moule married (in 1906), Hardy gave her a book of his poems as a wedding present. He gave Mr. Leslie a copy of *The Return of the Native*.

[2] Rebekah Owen and her sister Catherine were the 'good judges across the Atlantic' at whose 'instance' Hardy had (in 1895) restored the caged goldfinch to the pages of *The Mayor of Casterbridge*. Hardy's letters to Rebekah Owen have been published in *Hardy and the Lady from Madison Square* by Carl J. Weber (Waterville : Colby College Press, 1952).

## LETTER NO. 64

Max Gate. Monday.
[October 12, 1908.]

Dear E :

We are getting on here much as usual : a hammering all day : front door closed up, so that people have to come to the side door, even the most aristocratic (they do not mind at all, but seem rather to like it), and a general messiness outside, but nothing [messy] inside at all. The plastering *will not* get dry in your room, owing to the damp air : otherwise it could be finished. I do not suppose that it really will till next week. Would the first week in November be a good time for you to return ? On the 18th [of November] the day of the [*Trumpet-Major*] play [by A. H. Evans] a *Times* man, to whom I have offered a bed, will be sleeping here. I have told him of the alterations [now in process], but he will not mind.

You will be shocked to hear that Bosworth Smith died last Saturday evening, two hours after he had been brought home to Melcombe from London. He longed to be at home, but the doctors would not let him be moved till there was no hope : he would have died on the journey if the nurses had not injected strychnine. I suppose it was well to gratify his wish, but he must have suffered greatly by the way. He is to be buried on Thursday at Stafford.

Sir Elliott Lees died also last week — at the Royal Hotel, Weymouth, where he was taken ill on a speech-making tour. It was strange that *at last* we went to one of their parties, was it not : and how polite he was to you. Poor old Mrs. Lees who was so fond of him : how she must suffer.

I miss the psalm and chant tunes very much on Sundays, never hearing a note of music now.[1] Mr. Coutts the poet,

---

[1] In saying that he missed Emma's music, Hardy was quite sincere. She had played for him on the day he first saw her, March 7, 1870 ; two days

and a grandson of Coleridge, came to see me yesterday, and I went in to the Antelope [Hotel in Dorchester] to dinner with him. It rained in torrents. The cats are well, except Comfy, who has lost the use of one leg, and eats very little : I fancy he may not live much longer. But he is not unhappy, and purrs just the same as ever when stroked. Mrs. Baskett of Evershot wrote to ask us to lunch ; she was not sure whether you were come back, so wrote to me. I think of going (to-morrow) as it is very dull staying here alone.

I send on all that has come, except circulars etc.

Yours

T.

[P.S. :] Jane asks me to tell you that she is attending to the plants. There is going to be a change of proprietorship at the Broad Mayne baker's, and we think it unadvisable to do anything till you come : moreover Virgin is appointed baker of the stone-ground flour which Prideaux and others have laboured to re-introduce : and I want to try it.

### LETTER NO. 65

The Athenaeum, Pall Mall. S.W.

Tuesday [December 8, 1908].

Dear E :

I hope you understood my telegram of this morning. The jacket is that belonging to the grey-green suit that later, she and her sister had sung duets for him. After her death, when Hardy designed a tablet to be hung in the church at St. Juliot, he made special mention of the fact that she had there 'conducted the church music'. Half a dozen years after writing this letter to Emma, he penned a sketch of himself for publication in *Who's Who*, and there named, as one of his recreations, 'old church and dance music'. Shortly after his eighty-sixth birthday, when Sir John Squire called at Max Gate and brought the singer, John Goss, with him, Hardy got Goss to play and sing all of Emma Hardy's old songs, while the aged poet-novelist stood behind the piano-stool smiling through his tears and exclaiming 'Dear ! dear !' as he listened to the music.

you saw me wearing last summer, and the waistcoat is a knitted one — black and white. Herkomer began the portrait with these, and wants them to finish with.

I suppose I shall return Thursday. Do not send anything later than Wednesday night. I wonder if you will have sent off the right articles.

I don't much like the portrait. Cold and dry here.

Yours<br>T.

## LETTER NO. 66

The Athenaeum, Pall Mall. S.W.<br>Friday morning [July 9, 1909].[1]

Dear E :

I have just got your note, and the bundle of letters. I did not remember that I said definitely that I would return Wednesday, which will show you what a confusion I am in. But being now in a little back room at the hotel I am more comfortable, and can wait on for what I have been waiting for — [the operatic version of] *Tess*.

Before you get this you will see from the *Times*, etc., that the Opera is coming on next *Wednesday* (July 14) evening. Baron d'Erlanger, of whom I inquired, writes simultaneously to say the same thing, and asks what stalls I require. I can only think of two — one for you if you come, and one for myself. The fact is I don't know how many I am expected to ask for : as it is an opera, and not a play, so that *he* is the author, and not I (except remotely) I think I cannot decently ask for more.

The question now is, will you come ? The [West Central] hotel is so crowded that if you come there we should be obliged to have a front room, where the din is

---

[1] This is the only letter with a 1909 date addressed to Emma Hardy (or, if there were others written, the only one preserved by her). At the end of this year Hardy published *Time's Langhingstocks*, and inscribed a copy to 'Miss F. E. Dugdale'.

terrific, and having given up my little back one I should not get it again. I think therefore that if you can possibly go to where you were last time, or [to] the Alexandra [Club], it would be safer. Moreover you would want to dress, and you could hardly do that at the West Central Hotel.

If you do decide to come you had better wire at once to the Alexandra, reply paid, and ask if you can have a room, or if they can get you one [elsewhere], for next Wednesday night.

They are all Americans nearly at the hotel.

You could of course, come up for that one evening, though it would be a fag.

I have no cheque book here — but will post on a cheque as soon as I get back to the hotel. Of course it doesn't really matter whether you have ready money or not down there. I did not know I had not given you any for this month. Henry would have let you have some in a moment.

If you feel absolutely disinclined to undergo the fatigue of coming you will be able no doubt to hear the Opera later.[1]

The Baron says that there have been so many catastrophes and delays connected with his opera that he determined not to say a word about it till now it is actually announced.

If you come, better not let the servants send on any letters at all.

I was thinking of returning to-morrow if this had not happened.

Yours

T.

[P.S. :] I am sending back some papers I don't want, and have written 'not to be forwarded' on them.

[1] Mrs. Hardy did come, and heard the opera.

## LETTER NO. 67

West Central Hotel,
Southhampton Row,
London, W.C.
Friday evening [April 22,] 1910.

Dear E :

I have been hunting for flats and lodgings for three mortal days. I did not intend to go into the matter so thoroughly, but having begun I could not help going on.

In flats, the difficulty is of course, the catering and service. All good flats in which this is supplied are central — say, not far from Charing Cross and Westminster. In Artillery Mansions, Victoria Street, Westminster, there is one on the sixth floor (with good lift) which I think might do. In Buckingham Gate, not far off is one on *ground* floor. It would suit you eminently, as you walk straight in. But then, it is rather dark : and is it healthy to sleep on the ground floor ? Whitehall Court, close to Charing Cross has excellent service, appointments, etc. but the price is high £8/8/- per week. The others are about four or five guineas.

Now for lodgings. I have found *excellent* apartments at 15 Quex Road, West Hampstead (as they call it, though it is really Kilburn). It is only a few steps from Kilburn High Road and would be very convenient for vehicles. I send a photograph. If the distance out is not objectionable it is far the most suitable place for us. The drawing room will be empty in about a fortnight. Service good — and furniture. Drawing Room and two bedrooms 2 guineas : also dining room £4. There is a bath room — etc.

I am going to look a little farther : but of course you have to decide. This, and the having to vote at Athenaeum, will keep me into next week. It is very cold here —

like January : but I have no influenza as yet. Address Athenaeum as usual.

Yours,<br>T.

[P.S. :] I have done *nothing* besides this — not even been to a theatre.

LETTER NO. 68

The Athenaeum, Pall Mall. S.W.<br>Wednesday [April 27, 1910].

Dear E :

I have nearly taken the Blomfield Court flat (Maida Vale), first floor. It would suit as to size and it may be the one you saw. It is very cheerful — and has an open view. The agent will reduce it from four guineas to four pounds. I have told him that if you approve I will have it from Wednesday next [May 4th] till the middle of July.

Now for the objections — this rent does not, I think, include plate and linen. But the Company (of whom I should take it) supply such, and I think I might get that included. The woman who attends to the flats would bring in breakfast, if necessary — and there is a restaurant *close* by. We could manage, I am sure, as to food — between restaurant, housekeeper, and clubs.

But this has occurred to me since leaving the agents — who will open the door of an afternoon ? No doubt we could hire a person for, say, one afternoon a week, if you had people coming. But on the other days ? As there are three bedrooms we could have a parlour maid, like Daisy, who would get breakfast and tea. But would she come ?

The flat is rather larger than we want — something like the Ashley Gardens one with a nice entrance-hall — and has dining room, drawing room and kitchen. But I find that the little stuffy ones are 3½ guineas — or at lowest 3, and where catering is done they expect you to take nearly all the meals in.

If you feel strongly against taking it, or taking a flat at all, I don't, of course, mind. But let me know by return [post], as I promised them.

I don't know if you are coming up to the private view, Friday. I am rather tired.[1]

T.

[P.S. :] I am sending back a book that you forwarded — as it burdens me here — I direct it to you that there may be no mistake.

T.

## LETTER NO. 69

The Athenaeum, Pall Mall. S.W.
Saturday [April 30, 1910].

Dear E :

I have looked at the Flat at Blomfield Court again to-day, and have told the agents that I will give a final answer on Monday afternoon. The drawing room is not *excellently* furnished, but as good as we shall get : the dining room looks very well. The agent says that linen and silver will be supplied (indeed it is in the flat now) but suggests that we should bring a little linen — such as towels or napkins I suppose he means. I think that the plated silver teapot should be brought — I think we might do without the urn.

Unless you write to say on second thoughts you do not want it, but would rather go to the seaside etc. I will take it on Monday. He undertakes to have it ready by *Thursday* — so I suggest your coming up that day.

I think I will run down and fetch any more things I require, when we are settled in — as I cannot say now.

Yours T.

[1] Hardy was now approaching his seventieth birthday.

P.S. I don't know where to direct this, as you don't say how long you stay at Bournemouth. I will write the chief points in duplicate, and send one letter to Bournemouth — and the other to Max Gate.

I went to the Private View, and saw the usual people. There is no great picture [in the Exhibition this year].

The agent says a woman can be called in to clean the kitchen, etc. Shall I get somebody to get all ready for you?

T.

[Second postscript :] The address of the flat is 4 Blomfield Court, Maida Vale — you must come [by] Great Western — 10.40 I think.

## LETTER NO. 70

The Athenaeum, Pall Mall. S.W.<br>Monday : noon [May 2, 1910].

Dear E :

Immediately on the receipt of your letter this morning I wrote off to Snells, the agents, making my definite offer for the flat — I should have called personally on them, but it is so very wet, and they wanted, too, the offer in writing. I imagine they will accept it — and as soon as I get their reply I will let you know. I told them we wished to enter Thursday, and they seemed to think there would be no difficulty. As, no doubt, you will like to know as soon as I do, I will wire their answer, unless it comes so late in the afternoon that I may just as well write.

Will you bring with you the striped shirt which was washed last week — the wide-striped one.

Yours<br>T.

[P.S.:] You will have seen in to-day's *Times* the text of the Parliament Bill — it will be a historical document. I

went to Gosse's to supper last night. Mrs. Gosse is going
to come and see us in the flat when she and Gosse return
from Italy in a fortnight.

T.

LETTER NO. 71

West Central Hotel,<br>
Southampton Row,<br>
London, W.C.<br>
Tuesday, 3 May 1910

Dear E :

You will have received my telegram to say that I have
definitely taken the flat (the address of it is 4 Blomfield
Court, Maida Vale, London N.W.) though I have not
actually signed the agreement. However the points are
settled and the signing is a form. Of course extras have
cropped up as they always do — one is £2 for linen for
the ten weeks — which means sheets, napkins, tablecloths
etc. I thought it best to hire the linen instead of bringing
our own : but if you would rather bring our own, they
will allow back the £2. My idea was that the sheets
would be heavy and troublesome to pack. I have ordered
in coals and wood, and the porter will light the fires
Thursday morning and he or his wife air the mattresses,
and bedclothes (on the assumption that we use theirs). If
you wire any time to-morrow that you wish to bring the
latter, I will tell him to air only the mattresses and blankets.

As I said in my telegram, I think Daisy should come
*with* you, as I may not go down [to Dorchester] for a week
or two, and if we are alone in the flat, and the weather is
wet, like yesterday's, it will be very awkward without
her. The spot is open — almost suburban — and she can
run out to the shops in Clifton Road, close adjoining, as
well as she can to the Dorchester ones.

Come Great Western to Paddington — either by the

10.41, which arrives 2.53, or by the 12.49, arriving at
4.10 — the latter is the quicker, and will be quite soon
enough. Write *here* when you get this, and say which
[train] — and if I am to meet you, or await you at the
flat. As I am rather worn out I should prefer the latter,
but of course will meet you if you would feel uneasy at
having to get cab yourself. You must have a four-wheeler,
as a taxy cannot carry baggage.

Will you arrange for paying Trevis next Saturday —
and the one following : I will get Henry to do so later on,
as I did last time.

If you post your letter here to-morrow any time
before the evening post goes it will be soon enough.

The flat people are going to find silver, though *what*
sort of silver I don't know. But don't bring the urn till
you have seen what they provide. The china etc. seems
fairly pretty. I would not, if I were you, bring any silver
except perhaps a few teaspoons.

If Thursday should be too soon, you must of course
come later. But I am *paying* from Thursday.

Yours,

\*   \*   \*      T.

[Mrs. Hardy duly arrived in London and for ten weeks they
occupied the Maida Vale flat. In mid-July their tenancy
ended and Mrs. Hardy then returned to Max Gate. Her
husband stayed on at the flat a few days longer, in order to
present himself on July 19 at Marlborough House to be in-
vested with the Order of Merit — an honour conferred upon
him in the preceding June. Before the date of the investiture,
Hardy sent two letters off to Max Gate.]

LETTER NO. 72

The Athenaeum, Pall Mall. S.W.<br>
Friday, 15:7:1910.<br>
[July 15, 1910.]

Dear E :

I am glad to hear that you got home safely, and are not, at any rate, any worse. If your cough does not disappear in a few days perhaps the sea-side would send it away ; but I would not go far, and certainly would not come back to London.

I manage very well at the flat now, though at first it seemed awkward. I go out to breakfast at the adjoining restaurant, and while I am out Mrs Smith the porter's wife (a gentle nice woman) comes and does my room, cleans boots, etc. I have all my other meals at the Club or elsewhere. I had to go to the city this morning, so I breakfasted on my way at one of Lyons's places opposite the Marble Arch. It was very pleasant — the view down Park Lane, the cool morning air blowing in, etc. The only time that is depressing is when I come home at 10 or ½ past, and go into the dark silent flat, full of the ghosts of all those who have visited us there. I do not think you would be able to stay at the flat during the few days I remain, as you would not have sufficient conveniences, and could hardly go out to breakfast, do without hot water, etc : and I am away nearly all day.

If I can get off on Tuesday afternoon I think I will run down to the sea somewhere for a day or two before coming home. So do not send on anything after *Monday evening's* post. Keep the Westminster Bank letter till I return, and any other bank or dividend letters.

Henry sends a post card saying that he *saw* Rolls, the aviator, killed at Bournemouth ! Put 'O.M.' *only*, on the envelope after my name.

T.

[P.S. :] Lady St. Helier wires to [invite] me to dine with her to-night : so I shall.

## LETTER NO. 73

4 Blomfield Court [Maida Vale]
Monday morning [July 18, 1910].

Dear E :

I send the study key herewith. Do not send any more letters, as I propose to return Wednesday afternoon at latest. I meant to come Tuesday (to-morrow) but I don't think I can get off by then. Instead of going to the sea for two or three days as I intended, before returning, I am [now] thinking of going there after being at home a few days. Lady St. Helier and others say I look fagged out. Miss Dugdale is coming this afternoon, if she can, or to-morrow, to see that I am all right, and to put things straight preparatory to my leaving and to [type]write some letters [for me].

I have no difficulty about breakfast. The porter's wife, Mrs Smith, offered to bring up some, instead of my going out, so she does : she also says she will get me lunch or anything — if it should be too wet for me to go to the Athenaeum or elsewhere. So that between the two I am well looked after.

I think your chill will go off by degrees now that you are in the fresh air. I fancy you went out too much when you arrived, which may have caused a relapse.

Of course you must put off all the people who want to intrude by saying you are ill and I am away. I daresay there will be more later on.

Even when you open the study you will not be able to get at the urn, etc, as they are locked up in the cupboard, and I don't know what I did with the key of it. It is, however, of no importance, as you could easily explain : such things continually occur when people have been away : we sat on packing cases to tea at Lady St. Helier's once, I remember. Lord Curzon writes to ask me to sign an anti-suffrage letter which is to appear in the *Times*, signed by influential people ; but of course I shall not.[1] It does not rain this morning, but I think it will soon. I send on a letter separately that has just come.

T.

*   *   *

[On page 45 the reader has been allowed to look into the notes of Rebekah Owen and there read her observation that 'No action of Emma Lavinia's ever surprises me and probably does not her husband'. Emma's next action, however, would certainly have surprised Miss Owen, had she known about it. Mrs. Hardy turned to writing poems ! Shortly after Hardy's return to Max Gate with the 'O.M.' safely tucked after his name, the weather became bad and August proved extremely wet. When blue skies again reappeared, Mrs. Hardy wrote 'A Blue-day Orison'. The poem need not be quoted here in its entirety, since four lines will probably more than satisfy the reader's curiosity :

> With leaps and bounds the soul does run
> To greet this morn so lovely well begun,
> Filling the heart with high delight,
> To see so fair a morn so handsome bright.

[If it be true that no action of Emma's ever surprised Hardy and that he was not now surprised to learn that fair weather had moved his wife to write a poem, it was because he had had ten years' experience with the way the poetic sap flowed in her veins. He cannot have forgotten the day when her poem 'Spring Song' appeared in the pages of *The Sphere*. Hardy himself had contributed a poem to the very

[1] Hardy's 'of course' was said in deference to Emma's well-known interest in woman-suffrage. On February 8, 1907, she had marched in a suffragist parade in London.

first number of this new magazine ('At the War Office, London' appeared in the issue of *The Sphere* for January 27, 1900), and shortly thereafter Mrs. Hardy offered the editor, Clement K. Shorter, a poem of her own. The editor's embarrassment will be clear enough to any reader who will turn to the issue of *The Sphere* for April 14, 1900, and there read the wry comment on Emma's 'Spring Song' : 'We all know that Mr. Thomas Hardy began his literary career writing poetry. It is interesting to know that his wife has also written poems. Mrs. Hardy sends me the following verses, which I am happy, as one of the most enthusiastic admirers of her husband's books, to print in *The Sphere*.'

[When the *Graphic* printed 'The Darkling Thrush' (December 29, 1900), Mrs. Hardy promptly wrote *her* poem about the thrush. This poem has ten lines, but the reader will probably be satisfied to have me quote only four of them :

> There's a song of a bird in a tree, —
> A song that is fresh, gay, and free,
> The voice of a last summer's thrush,
> Shaking out his trills — hush ! hush !

Early in the new century, *The Academy* (to which Hardy had previously contributed) announced a competition in the writing of poems on the planting of a rose-bush. Among others, Eden Phillpotts submitted some lines. So did Emma Hardy. On April 27, 1901, *The Academy* printed her poem 'The Gardener's Ruse' with the editorial remark that 'This week Mrs. Thomas Hardy tells us in the following interesting lines how rose trees are planted in Wessex'. Her poem gave a twenty-line account of the Dorset habit of planting an onion near the roots of a rose-tree,—

> For the onion was bound to make roses sound,
> And a fine rich perfume to win.

[In addition to London magazines like *The Sphere* and *The Academy*, the local Dorchester newspaper, the *Dorset County*

*Chronicle*, was supplied with poetic effusions by Emma Lavinia. Hardy cannot have forgotten her poem entitled 'Dancing Maidens'. In *Tess* he too had written about dancing maidens, but he had certainly never composed anything like Emma's lines :

> . . . the gay little maids they danced all day,
> Though in grief for their mother — that was their way.
> 'O, mother come back, come back, come back,'
> They cried as they danced all three, alack !

She also wrote on 'The Trumpet Call' sounded by daffodils in March.

[Hardy cannot have forgotten all this ; nor did others. When Ford Madox Ford called at Max Gate and found Hardy out, Mrs. Hardy entertained him by reading 'her own innocuous poems'. Some of these poems were about her cats. Other visitors to Max Gate commented on the 'rather wry smile' they noticed on Hardy's face when these poetic efforts of his wife were mentioned.

[Rebekah Owen was doubtless right in saying that 'no action of Emma Lavinia's ever surprises . . . her husband', but there now followed one action that *did* surprise him. He knew nothing about it at the time. She began writing 'Some Recollections' — an autobiography, 'of the existence of which he was unaware till after her death' (*Early Life*, p. 96). On the last page, which she reached on January 4, 1911, she summarized her life thus : 'I have had various experiences, interesting some, sad others. . . .' (This was the manuscript which the second Mrs. Hardy, in the remark quoted above on page vi, called a 'diary'. The surviving part of the autobiography, edited by Evelyn Hardy and Robert Gittings, was published in 1961.)

[Five months later, Mrs. Hardy received at Max Gate the last letter which Hardy ever wrote her — 'last', on the assumption that she kept all the letters he wrote her in 1911.]

## LETTER NO. 74

The Athenaeum, Pall Mall. S.W.
Saturday [June 10, 1911].

Dear E :

I have just received the letters you sent yesterday : also your note. I think of returning [home] about next Thursday : I was coming sooner, as I am beginning to feel fatigued, but Mrs. Crackanthorpe, on whom I casually called, wants me to go with her to a play (I don't know what it is about) next Wednesday afternoon : and as she has bought the tickets I must stay over [until] then.

It is cold and wintry here. I did not bring my ordinary walking greatcoat — only that long waterproof : so I have to walk about in it, having nothing else. I think the weather is changing to wet.

Mrs Crackanthorpe, also Lady St. Helier, are going away Coronation week [June 22, 1911] to avoid what the former calls 'the Coronation circus'. I am glad I decided not to be there.[1] I am not quite sure if I shall go on Monday night to that reception — not if I feel tired, but I can go by tube and back.

I met Lady Lewis accidentally in the street, and she has asked me to lunch. She is such an amiable woman I think.

I should not be able to stand the knocking about the streets — which one cannot avoid doing — if I did not eat more than I do at home. I try to do this. I thought the warm weather would not last.

T.

[P.S. :] Post letters up to *Monday night* — not later.

\*     \*     \*

[1] Hardy went to the Lake District with his brother Henry.

[Mrs. Hardy observed what her husband had called 'the Coronation circus' by composing a poem entitled 'God Save Our Emperor King'. She arranged her lines as antiphonal stanzas, in a dialogue carried on by 'India' and 'Great Britain'. She was apparently pleased enough with her work to use it as the final poem in the collection of her verses which she made before the close of the year 1911. In 1909 Hardy had collected *his* poems — 94 of them, composed over a period of forty years or more — and had published them in *Time's Laughing-stocks*. Now, in December 1911, she 'published' *her* poems, by getting F. G. Longman, the Dorchester stationer (Hardy mentions him in Letter 44), to print a little book of them for her. She entitled the book *Alleys*, but what that title means is by no means clear.

[And now that her 'Recollections' were complete and her *Alleys* 'published', Mrs. Hardy was ready for a more ambitious project. In 1912, while her husband was busily occupied with new prefaces, new revisions, and new proof-reading required for the *Wessex Edition* of his collected works (twenty-four volumes, published by Macmillan & Company, 1912–1931), she wrote her 'Exposition of Great Truths by a New Treatment' and in 1912 'published' it under the title *Spaces*. Once again, the faithful Dorchester stationer, F. G. Longman, put her work into print. Since it is likely that few readers of the present volume have ever had a chance to read Emma Hardy's 'Exposition of Great Truths', a brief account of it may be given here. The book is divided into four parts. Part 1 deals with 'The High Delights of Heaven', where there will be 'ease of locomotion — whether by wings or otherwise'. Part 2 is about 'Acceptors and Non-Acceptors', and describes 'the plan of Salvation prepared to rescue many . . . from Satan's power. . . .' Part 3 is about Hell; it gives a vivid description of 'the Last Day . . . when suddenly a spot of light will appear in the East at 4 o'clock A.M. according to western time — and dark night of Eastern time or about that hour . . . and . . . bodies will be seen rising and floating in the phosphorescent great oceans. . . .' Part 4 is entitled 'Retrospect'. In her 'Recollections' Mrs. Hardy had declared : 'I have some philosophy and mysticism', and there can be no doubt about the fact that *Spaces* gives an eloquent 'exposition' of what 'mysticism' meant to her.

[On November 24, 1912, Emma Hardy doubtless 'celebrated' her seventy-second birthday with little help from her husband. The sixteenth volume in the definitive 'Wessex Edition' — *The Hand of Ethelberta* — was just about to appear, with a new preface which Hardy had written in the previous month. Three days later, at seven o'clock on the morning of the day when the Dorchester Dramatic Society was to give a performance of *The Trumpet-Major*, Mrs Hardy died. There would be no more letters to the woman who had once been his 'dearest Emmie'.]

# EDITORIAL EPILOGUE

WHEN death puts an end to a correspondence, an editor is tempted to let the curtain fall without further words. 'The rest is silence.' How easy it is to quote Hamlet's perfect valedictory !

In Hardy's case, however, the rest is *not* silence. In the months immediately following Emma's death, poem after poem poured from his heart. As soon as the disappointments and the irritations of the present were removed, Hardy's memory eagerly fell back upon the past 'when our day was fair'. He soon learned to overlook the rebukes and the insults, to forget the rudeness and the jealousy of recent years, and let his thoughts dwell on happier days when people had noticed the 'magic in my eyes' and had remarked on his 'radiance rare and fathomless'.

As Sir Arthur Quiller-Couch has observed, all who knew Hardy in his later years were reverently aware that he constructed a pure fairy-tale of that youthful time [the years of his Cornish romance, 1870–74], bathed in romantic colour, and that it took only a word from a friend or a sight of a familiar scene to set him off retracing, reclothing, reliving the happy events of his dream. (*Hardy of Wessex*, p. 173.)

Once again Emma became 'the woman whom I loved so, and who loyally loved me'. Before she had been dead a year, Hardy had written dozens of poems about her.

When (having been elected an Honorary Fellow of Magdalene College) Hardy went to Cambridge in November 1913 to be 'installed', he told A. C. Benson, the President of Magdalene, that he (Hardy) had written some poems about his wife, but didn't know whether he ought to publish them or not. They were 'very intimate, of course — but the verses came ; it was quite natural ; one looked back through the years and saw some pictures ; a loss like that makes one's old brain vocal !'

Hardy finally decided to give them to the world, and in 1914 he published the twenty-one 'Poems of 1912–13' in *Satires of Circumstance, Lyrics, and Reveries*. Into these verses he had distilled the quintessence of his memories of the past, and (later on) he published other poems on the same subject. In *Hardy of Wessex* I remarked : 'There are nineteen [others] which should be read in this connection. . . . There are, then, forty autobiographical poems in which Hardy's Cornish romance is tenderly enshrined.' It is now clear that there are many more than forty. Hardy's poems about Emma were published over a period of thirty years, 1898–1928, and they have never been brought all together and given the unified presentation they deserve. The present editor is, as he has already remarked, now engaged in compiling such a collection and hopes shortly to be able to present readers with a volume of English poetry which will, he thinks, surprise them with its richness and variety, its poignancy and charm, and its wistful beauty. That projected volume must remain the chief reason for the publication of the present volume of letters. For, to understand the poems in all their subtleties and ramifications, it is necessary to understand the poet who wrote them. These letters help us to achieve that understanding.

Specifically, as we look back over these seventy-four letters, what *do* they tell us ? Many things, of course ; some of more importance than others. Among the little facts that seem to have left no record elsewhere are 'Becky' Owen's turning Catholic, Major-General Henniker's reason for reading Byron, Osgood's 'sad' funeral, Rider Haggard's trip to Mexico, Hardy's 4 a.m. search for a lost cat, and the 'saving' of the American copyright in *Tess*. More important, however, are these gains :

(1) We learn a great deal about the nature of the man who wrote these letters — his patience, his forbearance, his humility. True, he could be parsimonious and could talk about saving sixpence ; true, he did not say 'please' or 'thank you' very often. But his traits of character are, in general, attractive, and it is clear that those misguided persons who have turned to *Cakes and Ale* for their picture of Hardy have been woefully deceived. For the past thirty-five years, one of the most frequently repeated questions asked by curious readers has been : How much truth is there in Somerset Maugham's novel ? *Cakes and Ale* was published just two years after Hardy's death. In this novel Herbert Driffield was obviously patterned after Thomas Hardy, but no attempt was made to indicate where fact ended and fiction began. Hardy himself had once remarked that this way 'of getting lies believed about people . . . is a horror to contemplate'. In view of the grotesque misrepresentations in *Cakes and Ale*, it is clear that the letters in the present volume acquire unusual importance. Also, that no publication of mere excerpts from the letters would serve. It would not do to pick a sentence here and a phrase there, and indicate omissions with a dot-dot-dot. That procedure would have only suggested to the inquisitive reader of the Maugham novel that something revealing had been left out. The letters here are therefore published in full, with all of their occasional pettiness. The character of the writer comes through in spite of the trivialities.

(2) These letters make it clear that I was wrong in a

previously-published comment on Hardy's social proclivities. In *Hardy of Wessex* I wrote about

> Mrs. Hardy's . . . very feminine delight in polite society. She liked to meet people. . . . She liked to entertain and to be entertained. . . . The social engagements multiplied. Hardy himself got very little out of them. . . . He was glad to slip away as soon as possible. . . . Hardy yielded to the demand for society on the part of his wife.

The letters now printed clearly demonstrate that this aspect of my earlier picture was false. Hardy himself was the one who 'liked to be entertained'. It is clear now that Emma often remained at home at Max Gate. When he was alone in London, Hardy was quite ready, at a moment's notice, to accompany Mrs. Crackanthorpe to the theatre, to be summoned to the dinner-table of Lady St. Helier, or to the tea-table of the Duchess of Abercorn. These letters show how incredibly willing he was to waste his time. In short, *he* was the socially-minded one. Not that Emma was 'anti-social': she wasn't. But it is clear that she had some reason for exploding to T. P. O'Connor about the way 'these women . . . in London Society' were 'poison' for Hardy.

(3) On the other hand, these letters make it clear that what Curator Moule called Emma's 'general unbearableness' (p. 45) was much greater than any reader of Hardy's poems might have supposed. Her abrupt departures for Calais, her impulsive cancellation of invitations to a garden party, her unannounced return home in 1900, her aches and pains, her lame knee and sprained ankle, her chills and influenza, her failing eyesight and her 'shingles', her general unpredictability, all are clearly brought out by the searchlight of these letters.

(4) We learn, too, how unreliable, at times, *The Early Life* and *The Later Years of Thomas Hardy* can be. In them he was, of course, trusting his memory, aided by his notes and his

letter-files. But he often went wrong. These letters to his
'dear Em' show that his memory could fail him, and that when
he *thought* he was at home in Dorset, he was really in London:
and that when he *thought* she was there in London with him,
she was really in Dorchester, or in Bournemouth, or elsewhere.
He did not always know where. Always 'mention the *town*
when you give your address' (Letter 47) !

(5) Finally, these letters give a quiet but eloquent demon-
stration of Hardy's innermost 'soul'. Let me explain what I
mean by this. In the last poem in *Late Lyrics* (1922) Hardy
represents himself as sitting before the Max Gate fire, reviewing
his own life. The crackling 'sticks' seem to be his own voice
speaking to him :

> 'You taught not that which you set about,'
>     Said my own voice talking to me ;
> 'That the greatest of things is Charity. . . .'

William Lyon Phelps interrupted the dialogue at this point
to remark (in *Scribner's Magazine*, November 1922, p. 630) :
'Well, if Hardy has not taught it, he has done something
better : he has expressed it in his daily life.' That is true.
One cannot read these letters to Emma without being impressed with their restraint, their forbearance, their 'charity'.
That he had his own faults is obvious enough. Even his
admirer Rebekah Owen knew that. 'I saw his faults,' she
once wrote, 'and talked and laughed over them with my sister :
but I would never admit them when his first wife dissected his
character, nor ever gossip about them to anyone' (*Hardy and
the Lady from Madison Square*, p. 196). But in Hardy's letters
there is no retaliatory dissecting of Emma's character. Instead,
behind the frequent triviality, one can sense what Robert
Browning called the

> Infinite passion and the pain
> Of finite hearts that yearn.

Hardy had that kind of yearning heart. On July 17, 1896, he received a letter from Jeannette L. Gilder, the American journalist. She had solicited an interview with Hardy — a request which he had denied. In her letter Miss Gilder remarked : 'I knew you were a great man, but I did not appreciate your goodness until I received your letter this morning.' That quality of 'goodness' shows up again and again in Hardy's letters to Emma, and no one who can read between the lines will fail to find it.

# INDEX

# Index

# Index

# Index

III

THE END

PRINTED BY R. & R. CLARK, LTD., EDINBURGH